Angel

CW01497193

By

David J Smith

The true story of Britain's most famous walking poles
and the Angels they carried

Live to Achieve
David Smith and probably many others

Cover picture – The Angel Poles on the sands at Prestatyn, Wales after the King Offa's Dyke 185mile run.

Cover photo design courtesy of Graeme and Toby at popi. www.popi.co.uk

Contents

Dedications

Prologue

Chapter 1. Finding an Owner

Chapter 2. The Pennine Way

Chapter 3. The Lakeland 100

Chapter 4. Hadrian's Wall

Chapter 5. Enduroman Double Ironman

Chapter 6. Enduroman Continuous Quintuple Ironman

Chapter 7. The Millennium Way

Chapter 8. Triathlon X

Chapter 9. The Yorkshire 3 Peaks (with SANDS)

Chapter 10. King Offa's Dyke

Chapter 11. My final journey

Epilogue.

The Individual Pole Angel Stories.

Chesterfield SANDS – The story so far.

Acknowledgements.

Dedications

This book is dedicated to the 70 Angels who travelled on the last journey of the poles, from Chepstow to Prestatyn. May they continue their adventures in lands far away.

Theo
Grace
Lily
Luke
Rosie
Esmaé Amelia
Adam
Poppy
Ruby
Lola
Declan-Nathaniel
Georgia-Lauren
Nevaeh-Aaliyah
Brogan
Archie
Ashley Dean
Theo
Phoenix James
Violet
Lucy
Jak
Harrison
Archie
Raife
David Ezra
Leigha-Jade
Amiee-Grace
James
Riley Lomas
Kian
Sam

Joe

Ian

Austyn

Mia

Elsa Jane

Casey-Leigh

Jassy

Nathaniel

Teegan

Kiara

Isla

Danita Jay

Baby Servante

Joshua

Benjamin-John

Jacob

Charlie

Jack

Emma-Jane

Isla-Grace

Jacob

Travis Peter

Lucy Elizabeth

Jesse

Baby Steveson

Henry

Leona Marie

Baby Cowdrey

Zowie Louise

Caleb George

Tia Rose

Poppy

Ryan Aaron

William Roy

Ashley

Ruby Jayne

Aaron

**Sasha
Flyn**

Prologue

A person who never made a mistake never tried anything new –
Albert Einstein

In September 2016 I took part in a running event called King
Offa's Dyke, a 185 mile continuous run along the English
Welsh border. It was the longest run I had ever attempted and
due to the length and severity of the terrain, I took along my
walking poles. Little did I know at the time how significant
this run was going to be. These walking poles went from total
obscurity to having their picture shared on Facebook over
29,000 times, as well as appearing in several newspapers. All
this happened due to two things:

1. The poles were covered with the names of babies born
    sleeping or who died shortly after birth. Let's call them the
    Pole Angels.

2. On the journey home after the event I accidentally left the
    poles and their Angels on a train.

Extensive enquiries failed to find the poles so, as a last resort, I
turned to Facebook for help. The response was overwhelming
and humbling. Thousands were touched by what had
happened and many went out of their way to try and find
these lost poles. Suddenly the Pole Angels were being shared
all over the UK and then all over the world.

As owner and loser of the poles, I felt the full story should be
told. What now follows is my account of the life of the poles,
from humble beginnings in a Decathlon store to taking part in
some of the longest and toughest triathlons and runs in the
UK. It is told through the eyes of the poles (if poles do have
eyes). It culminates in the poles final journey on the King

Offa's Dyke run. All views expressed are those of the poles and are as accurate as the poles are aware.

Finally, and most importantly, I have asked each Pole Angel family if they would like to share their story and write about how their Angel ended up on the poles. These true stories tell of the harsh realities encountered with still birth and neonatal death.

A short history of Chesterfield SANDS, the work it does and contact details are given at the end of the dedications.

This is the first book I have written. I hope you enjoy reading it. I hope it will evoke many emotions. I have given contact details in the epilogue if you would like to contact me about any aspect of the book.

All profits from this book will go to Chesterfield SANDS. By reading this story you are not only helping the charity continue its vital work, but you are making sure the Pole Angels are never forgotten.

Thank you.

Chapter 1.

Finding An Owner

If people concentrated on the really important things in life, there'd be a shortage of walking poles – adapted from Doug Larson

Now let's get something sorted right from the start. I am a pair of poles. Diosaz 700 Raid Team Quechuo to give you my proper name. I am straight and true, sleek and elegant. I am not a pair of sticks. I did not come from a tree, I am not crooked and curved and I'm not much use if you want to make a fire.

Don't get me mixed up with my Scandinavian cousins who are taking the UK by storm. I don't have fancy handles, just plain cork for me and my tips aren't at a weird angle either. On the plus side you don't have to have lessons to use me like you do with Nordic walking poles, if you believe all the hype.

Now I'm glad we have cleared that up. I don't mind the term "walking" or even "trekking" in front of me, after all that's what my owner used to do with me most of the time, although he did tell others he was running and would call them running poles. The other name which has been used to describe me is "cheating sticks". I find this highly offensive. It is the endurance athletes who would not consider using me that have coined this phrase. They are highly tuned racing snakes who can run mile after mile at pace with minimal exertion and make it look effortless. My owner certainly does not fall into that category. He realised many years ago that his body, particularly his knees, had limitations. He had run several marathons but the after effects would be knee pain.

This limited the amount of running he could do without causing serious injury. He turned to cross training to supplement his exercise regime, swimming and cycling regularly and this led him into the world of triathlons. However he loved his running and he had bigger plans than marathons. He wanted to go further, much further, and this is where I, the walking poles, come in.

I was born, well actually made, well hand crafted with precision and skill in Italy. I was fortunate to be chosen to have a fluorescent green coating to my upper body, so I stood out compared to my brothers and sisters who had a demur, boring colour. But my destiny lay many hundreds of miles away in the UK. I did enjoy the Italian weather, the stylish clothing and the animated language. So it was quite a shock to be packed into the back of a lorry together with my sisters and brothers and transported across Europe and the English Channel to England. Initially we went to a huge warehouse. It was great fun. We were left alone all day. At night when all the humans had left we would play and dance together. These were happy days but they did not last long. One by one our numbers would go down as my fellow poles were removed from the warehouse, never to return.

It was barely a month after arriving that I was on my travels again to a place called "Nottingham". I was in a consignment of ten pairs of poles which were delivered early one morning to the Decathlon store in the city. This was quite different to the warehouse we had left. It had bright lights and loads of people wandered around staring at us, or feeling us, or even walking with us.

We got no rest at all. I knew any day I would be whisked away to a new life. I dreamed that maybe I would go to the Himalayas and climb Mount Everest or trek through unexplored jungles in South America. Then reality set in as I was currently in Nottingham, but there was no harm in dreaming.

One day a smartly dressed man came along and started to stare at me and my companions with great interest. He proceeded to pick up each and every pole on sale and examine us in infinite detail. I think he was pretending to be some kind of expert in the field of walking poles.

This guy was obviously not great at making a quick decision or parting with his own money because he disappeared briefly then returned with a beautiful lady, who must have been his wife. After a few words of wisdom from his wife, Ann, he lifted me from the racks and examined me for a ridiculously long time. He checked everything from my cork handles, my snug fitting straps, my two-piece aluminium shaft (continually using the internal locking mechanism to change my length) and my baskets and steel points. Finally he walked me over to the till and purchased me. I had a new owner, David Smith.

Chapter 2.

The Pennine Way

The person who walks alone is likely to find himself in places no one has ever seen before – Albert Einstein

I soon discovered that my new owner had a unique style when it came to using me. He knew that I would take the pressure off his knees, so he decided that the harder he pushed me down the greater the effort of reducing the impact on his knees as he moved. This resulted in me being constantly stabbed into the ground as if he was trying to aerate the soil. His technique was pretty much the same when he was on Tarmac, only this time my shaft would quiver with the vibrations of the impact and the noise would attract strange glances from those around him. I felt so embarrassed but he wasn't bothered. I'm told he had run marathons dressed as Winnie the Pooh and Tigger so was used to attracting attention.

My owner had started doing long distance walks and up to 2006 he had walked a continuous route from Land's End to the start of the Pennine Way. This had included walking Offa's Dyke along the English Welsh border, where he had struggled to finish due to knee problems. Eight days after leaving Chepstow he finally hobbled into the finish at Prestatyn a day later than planned. He had not used poles so only had himself to blame. When will these humans learn that poles are the way to go?

This experience had taught him that he needed help and now he had me to compensate for his mortal weaknesses.

The Pennine Way was part of David's bigger plan to eventually walk from Land's End to John o' Groats. He wanted to walk the full 267 mile route in one go and allocated two weeks to complete it. It is regarded as Britain's best known and toughest national trail so I was looking forward to some great scenery. It would certainly beat spending days on end in the umbrella stand, especially as I didn't get on too well with the umbrellas. They always came back soaking wet or not properly rolled away so they took up all the room. When it was a windy day sometimes they never came back at all.

My owner has many faults but he certainly believes strongly in preparation before any event. He had read many accounts about walkers quitting the Pennine Way just a few days after starting as the first section is probably the toughest. He was also very aware of his poor navigating skill. He could get lost in a supermarket if he didn't take care. So to ensure the trip was successful we went out on several walks to suss out the terrain.

On one such foray we were joined by Bengi, his toy poodle. We climbed out of Edale and up to the Kinder escarpment. It wasn't long before we were in thick mist with only a few metres of visibility. It was scary stuff and I'm sure we went round and round in circles before finding a route back off Kinder. By this time Bengi was looking more like a drowned rat than a pedigree toy poodle. David was quite alarmed at what Ann was going to say when he arrived home, so he did his best to bring Bengi back to life using the car heaters as a hair dryer.

On another occasion, when pushed for time, we set off at silly o'clock to check out Bleaklow Head and Wild Boar Clough. It was dark when we left the car and it wasn't much lighter when we returned a few hours later. I'm not sure how successful the route finding was but he seemed happy enough and I was grateful we hadn't got hopelessly lost again.

It was to be the summer of 2006 when we set off for my biggest walk ever, along the Pennine Way to Kirk Yetholm. David had packed next to nothing in his rucksack, as was customary for him. He always said as long as he looked half decent so he got let in to his accommodation for the evening then that was good enough. After all, he was unlikely to meet anyone who knew him and he wasn't going for an interview. He believed in taking only bare essentials, as a heavy rucksack was only going to hinder his progress and he liked to describe himself as a gazelle rather than an elephant. I like to think of myself as a cheetah, born for speed.

The journey did not start too well. He had planned to cover 40 miles the first day, from Edale to Mardsen, so we needed an early start. The taxi booked for 5.30am did not arrive so, after waiting 15 minutes, another taxi was booked and eventually arrived just after 6am. Being a very impatient person when we arrived at Edale we set off at a blistering pace, which was bordering on a run. I was having difficulty taking in all the beautiful countryside around me as I was bashed into the ground each step of the way. The taxi may have been late but there was no need for him to take his frustration out on me. On a section of the path near the Snake Pass, where there is a wooden board walk to prevent erosion, he jabbed my right side between two planks of wood in such a forceful manner that I became stuck. He had to return to me then pull with all his gazelle like force to extract me from between the wooden slats. After that small mishap he settled down a little and the walk became much more enjoyable.

The weather was glorious with not a cloud in the sky. My bright green colour glinted magnificently in the sunlight. David however was suffering in the heat and soon after midday he was out of water. Luckily at the A635 road crossing, 10 miles from Marsden, there was an ice cream van and he was able to rehydrate.

David had wanted to get to his B&B in Marsden by 4pm as it was the quarter finals of the World Cup in South Africa, and England were playing Portugal. He achieved his goal running the last few miles into the town. It was just unfortunate that England did not achieve their goal. In fact no team scored in normal time or extra time so it came down to penalties. England's atrocious record continued in major competitions as they lost the penalty shootout.

Naturally I was disappointed as I knew I would be in for another day of vicious stabbing tomorrow as David took out his disappointment on me. At least I spent the night in a nice warm bedroom as opposed to a draughty garage, which I was more used to.

The rest of the walk continued in glorious weather with not a drop of rain apart from one day. The daily mileages were a lot shorter than day one, so we could start at 9am and finish by 4pm and have an hour for lunch. Each day's accommodation had been booked in advance (David believed in good preparation) and consisted of B&B's and Youth Hostels (David believed in saving money). For most of the way it was just me and David and we would marvel at the outstanding beauty of the different landscapes we were passing through. From the vast Limestone crags at Malham Cove and the limestone pavement to the mighty High Force waterfall near Middleton-in-Teesdale, where the water cascades down 22m. But the highlight was the stunning canyon of High Cup Nick, which words can't describe. If I had lungs it would have taken my breath away. It made you glad to be alive. Maybe that trip to Nottingham Decathlon was not a bad choice after all.

One of the funniest moments of the walk came at Top Withens, Wuthering Heights country. David had noticed a few other walkers behind him and was determined not to be overtaken. He is so competitive it's unreal. He quickened his pace and when the other walkers were not in eye sight he would pick me up and we would run, just to make out we were actually really fast walkers. This tactic was working well until he forgot to check the map and we went totally off course. All of a sudden the other walkers were no longer behind us. Luckily he soon realised his mistake and we got back on track, but this time the roles were reversed. The other walkers were ahead and David kept his distance so they were none the wiser about our navigational faux pas.

A little disgruntled, we stopped at Top Withens and I was stabbed into the ground, as was customary. I'm not sure what was wrong with just propping me up against a wall. I guess it's a human macho thing.

Anyway, out came David's packed lunch, carefully prepared by the Youth Hostel the night before and David was soon tucking into his corn beef sandwiches (this was a youth hostel packed lunch, not M&S).

Now I thought sheep were vegetarians but this is not true. In just a few minutes David became surrounded by a herd of very hungry sheep. I guess they had given up on grass many years ago after being visited by walkers with much tastier food. The deadly pack of sheep encircled David and went into attack mode as they fought to get at the sandwiches. It was a close run thing as to who would be victorious in the battle, with both sides determined to win at all costs. In the end it was probably a draw, with the sheep managing to take some of the spoils of the sandwiches and David and I had to retreat to eat on the move.

Another hilarious moment occurred in the Cheviot Hills. David was already in an apprehensive mood, having seen Ministry of Defence signs saying "Danger. Do not touch anything as it may explode and kill you." We had seen fighter jets whizzing over our heads on many occasions so it was nothing out of the ordinary to see another one. However on this particular occasion I think the jet must have been a little closer to the ground and a little noisier than the rest. It was also very sneaky, coming in directly behind us so we never saw it coming. It flew directly over us, then, as David's eyes were just making out what was directly above him in the sky, the deafening roar of the engines hit us. I've never seen him jump so high. It was hilarious and if he hadn't got his hands in my straps I would have been tossed into the air as he pranced around like a demented chicken. Money can't buy moments like that – priceless.

Another priceless moment came at the end of the walk. David had cut drastically back on clothes to reduce the weight he had to carry. He basically had two T-shirts, both of which were England football tops. Now normally that would not be a problem in England, however he had forgotten that the walk may have started in England but it finished in Scotland. How embarrassing when we reached journey's end at Kirk Yetholm. I don't think the Landlord of the Guest house was very impressed and he then decided to talk at length about England's penalty shoot-out with Portugal, and how poor they were. David didn't dare mention that Scotland had failed to even make the finals.

The Pennine Way was successfully completed in the allocated two weeks. I did my job superbly, ensuring David's knees suffered no ill effects. The same could not be said for his feet which, by the end of the walk, had a lovely collection of blisters on them. At least by using me he was able to reduce the pressure on them as he walked. I saved the day. I was the unsung hero. He never mentioned me once on any postcards he sent home. Now there's gratitude for you. Never mind, I was looking forward to our next adventure together.

Chapter 3.

The Lakeland 100

It does not matter how slowly you go as long as you do not stop –
Confucius

The Lakeland 100 or Ultra Tour of the Lake District is
described by the organiser as the most spectacular long
distance trail race that has ever taken place within the UK. It
starts in Coniston and takes in the Dunnerdale fells, Eskdale,
Wasdale, Buttermere, Keswick, Matterdale, Haweswater,
Kentmere, Ambleside and Elterwater before returning to
finish at Coniston. Although the route does not pass over any
Lakeland summits it still has 6856m of ascent. Competitors
have 40 hours to complete the 105 mile course and less than
half finish due to the tough terrain and tricky navigation.

David had seen an advert in his running magazine in January
2009 for the Lakeland 100. The organisers also ran a 50 mile
race, which basically was the 2nd half of the Lakeland 100
route. There was still 2965m of ascent and a 24 hour time limit.
David thought the 50 would be ideal preparation for the 100
the following year. I was grateful to finally get out of the
house. David had travelled out to the Sahara earlier in the
year, leaving me behind, so the Lakeland 50 was my chance to
show him what I was capable of. It would be the longest race
of my career so far. David had previously completed a mind
numbing 24 hour track race a few years earlier, clocking 92
miles but with a total ascent of 0 metres the track marathon
would have been infinitely easier and the navigation a lot
simpler.

David and his wife, Ann, spent a week in June 2009 in the
Lake District. David and I would be out at the crack of dawn

covering sections of the course. Then later in the day David would leave me behind and he and Ann would go out to a different section of the course. By the end of the week David had covered the majority of the route and I had done about half of it. David was hoping to follow other competitors for at least the first stage. He was a cunning character. On paper he decided it would take between 10 and 12 hours to complete the race, so not too much would be in the dark. That sounded good to me, as I knew David would probably get lost in the dark.

In August 2009 we lined up for the Lakeland 50. Few competitors had poles like me. When the race started everyone seemed to go running off at a crazy pace. David and I were initially left at the back. This had the unfortunate effect that David increased his pace, stabbing me into the ground in a quicker rhythm than I was expecting. By checkpoint 2 we were an hour up on David's schedule. It felt great at the time but we had to pay for this over-exertion. We slowed dramatically as David struggled to keep going. Had it not been for the 2nd and 3rd placed ladies who David met up with at Langdale we would have struggled to break 12 hours. However, we all stayed together to the end and finished in 11 hours 28 minutes. If you had asked David to carry on and run another 50 miles after he had finished he would have had no chance. I was eager to continue. Bring on the Lakeland 100.

The 50 did teach David a few important lessons:-

1. Stick to your schedule and don't be drawn into going faster, especially in the early stages.

2. The camaraderie between competitors is fantastic, takes your mind off your aches and pains and lets the miles pass more quickly.

3. At night 3 people navigating is better than 1.

4. Whether it is day or night, he can't navigate.

5. You can go through a roller coaster of emotions during a long race, so you must be mentally prepared.

The pain of the 50 soon faded from David's memory and by October 2009 he was signing up for the 2010 Lakeland. It was a good job he did, as I had really enjoyed the spectacular scenery on the Lakeland 50 and wanted to see more.

David and I managed a couple of 30 mile training outings in the Peak District. One of them was a 35 mile route called "Toms Golden Miles", which had been set up as a charity walk by one of David's customers at the pharmacy. David and I started the run on a Saturday afternoon at 3pm and finished just after midnight. This meant that David got some good experience navigating in the dark. He had very wisely purchased a Satmap hand held satellite navigation device, without which we would have got hopelessly lost at night. I was certainly getting more confident that we would succeed. David, however, was still unsure and looking for every possible advantage he could get. About 4 weeks before the event he heard about a local hypnotherapist trainee who was looking for guinea pigs. He signed up for two sessions and had positive thoughts drilled into my head by the hypnotherapist. They got him to focus on memories of previous races when he had run well and felt strong. He would then visualise reaching the half way point of the Lakeland 100 feeling fresh and full of energy and ready to complete the 2nd half, which he knew he could do as he had previously completed it the year before. The hypnotherapist got him to select a trigger to bring these positive thoughts into focus. By touching the trigger he would feel the positive energy come into his body, banishing negative thoughts.

David decided that touching his wedding ring would be the trigger, as getting married was certainly the most important and positive life event he had ever experienced. Personally I can't understand why he didn't have me as the trigger. The hypnotherapy certainly made David feel more confident about the event. I was glad the therapist didn't get him walking round the room pretending to be a chicken.

Race day weekend finally came. David decided to make the whole pre and post-race ordeal as stress free as possible. We all left Chesterfield on Thursday evening and travelled up to a Travelodge on the M6, although I never made it out of the car boot. Then after a relaxing lie in on the Friday morning, for some, we all travelled the remaining 40 miles to Coniston to register for the race at 10am.

The organizers were very safety conscious and one of the first things that they did was to weigh each competitor. The weighing certainly focused David's mind on eating and drinking as much as possible during the event. He is so lucky that I am low maintenance.

There was also a mandatory kit check and unlike other competitors who had cut corners (since when has a pair of ladies tights constituted a body covering) David had taken extra kit for safety and comfort. As well as a spare base layer he had a lightweight fleece. He took a balaclava for his head and arm warmers, as worn by cyclists. (I think he was expecting snow). He chose to run in a short sleeve cycling top. This is something he has done for a few years as he likes the back pockets. Into these went his arm warmers, spare food, camera and any other items to prevent him from having to go into his rucksack too often. He carried a small supply of food freezer bags so any food, such as cake taken from a checkpoint, which he did not want to eat there and then, could be put into a bag then stuffed into a back pocket. Having me, his trusty poles, meant that his hands were always full so cycling jersey pockets were a big help. He chose running tights (proper tights and not ladies tights as worn by ladies and bank robbers) instead of shorts. He knew from training that he could run in them in hot weather. However David does feel the cold, so as the race started late afternoon he didn't want to have to change should it get cold overnight.

David previously marked the entire route on 1:20,000 OS maps in small strip sections. This had taken him hours to do. The route description, as provided by the organizers, was then added and the resulting maps laminated. He managed to get each half of the route on to 3 A4 maps. He therefore had to carry three maps to Dalemain at half way then swap them over to the next three maps. Each map had a hole punched into it and a shoe lace threaded through so it could be put around his neck. He used a lace colour code of red, white and blue laces so he could quickly tell which map he needed next. It sounded complicated but it worked well and kept his hands free for me. His Satmap GPS was carried on his rucksack chest strap. He would use the rechargeable battery to Dalemain then swap to lithium batteries to the end. He saved battery power by dimming the screen as much as possible and only turning the unit on when needed. If we lost power we would be doomed.

Ann, David's wife, was staying at Ambleside for the weekend. She had spent last year at Coniston for the Lakeland 50 and soon discovered there was not much to do there. Ambleside seemed a better option and, as the route passed through Ambleside after 89 miles, David would get to see Ann. He would probably be feeling pretty rough at this point, so Ann's smiling face would be the best possible sight to get his spirits up. Ambleside also had more shops for Ann to browse while she waited for David, although I don't think many were handbag shops.

After registration at Coniston, David and Ann drove the 8 miles to Ambleside and checked into the Ambleside Lodge. I stayed in the boot again. The hotel had a lovely big car park, so no problem with parking, which always seems to be the worst aspect of Ambleside. David managed to get a pasta meal down him in a local café then he went back to the hotel for an hours sleep, although with his mind buzzing about the race I'm not sure how much rest he actually got. Maybe he should have stayed in the boot with me. He certainly didn't like the idea of a 5.30pm start time.

We all drove back over to Coniston Race HQ for the pre-race briefing. Looking around the other competitors David tried to keep positive, even though they seemed more relaxed than me about the whole event. At least he had the best pair of poles going.

He gave in his bag for the half way point. He had basically packed a second rucksack, leaving absolutely nothing to chance, so if any part of his kit failed in any way he had a spare. Well that was nearly true. He hadn't packed a spare set of poles. He already had the best and I wasn't going to let him down. As long as he didn't lose me he would be fine, and there wasn't much chance of that.

After feeding his face again David and I lined up at the start, near the back. David was determined not to go off too quickly. When the gun went off we started walking. Everyone else seemed to be running and soon we were last, David stabbing me into the road as we followed the pack. I'm sure we were amusing the spectators as we clonked along at the rear. We kept everyone in sight and as the road turned into a track then started to climb, the runners ahead became walkers and we started to pass people. Who was laughing now?

David kept as relaxed as possible during the first leg. We needed to follow people as we did not know the route, but this was not a problem. We walked the whole way apart from a little trot into checkpoint 1 at Seathwaite. We were nicely on schedule. There were 14 checkpoints in all, with 3 being main feeding stations. For those checkpoints which were not main feeding stations David tried to enter and exit as quickly as possible, leaving me outside. A couple of cups of water and food to go, then he'd pick me back up and we would be on our way, hopefully a minute or so after arriving.

The next leg to Eskdale proved to be very muddy. I bet David was grateful for me as I kept him upright. Several runners around us hit the ground while tackling the slippery, boggy tracks. Four points of contact are always going to give better grip than two.

It was on this second leg that David and I paid the price for not navigating. The group we were following took a wrong turn. Nobody noticed until it was too late to turn back, so an alternative route was taken to get to the next checkpoint. We ended up crossing the River Esk, going over stepping stones. That would not have been so bad, however the majority of the stones were submerged. The river was running high and fast. I came to the rescue again, keeping David from slipping as he crossed.

The Eskdale checkpoint was again reached on schedule and again we spent as little time as possible there before starting stage 3. David was still on unfamiliar terrain, not knowing the route and needing to follow others, but there were still plenty of competitors around us. He aimed to get to Wasdale Head, checkpoint 3, before dark and we achieved it, although the checkpoint took a little finding.

So 19 miles were completed in 6 hours. David put his fleece and head torch on, ready for the night section. We had been keeping pace with two other runners, Anna and Alec, since Eskdale and David politely asked if he could join them for the next section. It seemed courteous to ask rather than to just follow. They were happy to let him join them and the three of them, plus me, set off up to Black Sail Pass with Anna leading the way.

In his practice walks David had not enjoyed the dark at all. I could tell by the way he tightened his grip on my cork handles. But now the fell-side was lit up with many head torches, the moon above us and runners in good spirits all around, chatting away. He was loving the whole experience. In fact, he was loving it too much. On the descent to Black Sail Youth Hostel we went ahead of Anna and Alec and started to pass others. David was at last on terrain he knew (well at least in daylight) and we were making good progress. I certainly helped David on the rough decent to Buttermere Lake and he ran into the checkpoint ahead of schedule. Alarm bells were ringing for me that our pace was too quick but David wasn't listening. We should have been slowing down and staying on schedule but David was on a high. We carried on at the same pace towards Braithwaite, checkpoint 5.

This section appeared to be particularly problematic to some, as we could see head torches in some very unusual places. David was grateful he had recced the route carefully before hand.

We were well ahead of schedule at the Braithwaite checkpoint (32 miles covered). David had been looking forward to this checkpoint as it was the first main feeding point, and it did not disappoint him. Two bowls of pasta, crisps and rice pudding were consumed instantly, as if he had never eaten in weeks and with no regard for table manners. He filled his camelback (water container) with water and orange for the first time since the start. 15 minutes later we were off again, keeping ahead of schedule.

On the section around the base of Skiddaw, then over to Blencathra David was tempted to cut the corner, even if it meant saving just a few 100 metres. There was no one around and it was still dark, but thankfully he decided against it. I didn't want to finish with a cheat.

David's walking style was starting to change and I guessed that his left foot was becoming sore due to blisters. At the start he had applied blister plasters to each foot in places where he was susceptible to blisters forming. At Blencathra, checkpoint 6 (41 miles), he decided to check his left foot out. The gel from the blister plaster was everywhere. It was as though the plaster had exploded. He removed as much as he could before applying another two plasters. Unfortunately the fool did not check his right foot, as it did not feel too bad. It's a good job I am low maintenance.

At the Blencathra Centre David met up with Andy. He appeared to be going through a bad patch. The two kept together more or less for the next two checkpoints, then Andy obviously recovered well as we never saw him again. This was a warning to David of the highs and lows of long races. Just get through the bad patches as best you can, they will not last forever.

As we progressed from Blencathra I could tell David's energy levels were starting to fall. Along the long section of the old coach road into Dockray his pace slowed such that we were walking most of the time, and we began to be passed by others. A group of three came by, Philip, Mark and Catherine, and David tried to keep up with them but their pace was too quick. They all looked in good shape and we did not expect to see them again.

It was at Dockray (checkpoint 7 - 49 miles) that David and I were passed by the eventual winner of the ladies race. Her pacing over the night sections was far better than ours and we never saw her again. It was an important lesson for David. Even pacing is the key. His little spurt over the night section was now costing us.

A couple of miles out of Dockray David ran out of drink. Great. The longest stage of 10 miles and he had nothing to drink. If only he had checked my Camelbak at the checkpoint. He soldiered on to Dalemain, walking the majority of the way, but I could tell his spirits were getting lower and lower. His left foot was starting to hurt again so I reckoned the blister plasters had not worked. His right foot was also hurting due to blisters, but as his first aid had not worked on the left foot he could not see the point of tinkering with the right. I'm not sure of the logic here. Surely he needed to attend to both feet immediately, but there's no telling some people. I had a horrible feeling he was going to find out about foot care the hard way. It's a good job my steel tips don't get blisters.

Dalemain (Checkpoint 8 – 59 miles) was our longest stop, approx. 20 mins. David was in a foul mood. He was grateful for the pasta the organisers were dishing up, but that was it. He was upset there were no chairs to sit on, upset there was no orange squash so he had to put just water in his Camelbak, upset no one could attend to his blisters. He wanted the earth but was not going to get it. The last straw was seeing others taking food out of their halfway kit bags and bottles of coke, and he had nothing. He had expected more food and drink options at the checkpoint. He had not prepared himself properly in this respect.

We set off from Dalemain and, as promised, David rang Ann to let her know where he was. He was in tears as he spoke to her. He should have been feeling great with half the race done, only half to go and his hypnotherapy kicking in. But he wasn't. Ann did her best to cheer him up and promised to be there at Ambleside. At that precise moment in time Ambleside seemed a long way away to David and dropping out seemed a good option.

At Pooley Bridge midway to the next checkpoint David went into a shop for provisions. They had Lucozade Sport, to his delight, and he carried on a lot happier, although a little disgruntled that his change weighed heavier than the £20 note he had originally started with. Then he met up with Philip. Philip was great and David was soon chatting away. His spirits were on the way back up. Philip explained how he had completed the Lakeland 100 in 2008 and 2009 and now he was on for a good time this year. David on the other hand was just thinking about finishing. 39:59:59 was good enough for him i.e. 1 second within the cut off time.

We arrived at Howtown (checkpoint 9 – 66miles) together and while Philip started on his second cup of tea David and I set off for Mardale Head. Up to this point we had enjoyed excellent weather. Now a fine drizzle started coming down, so on went the Gore-Tex. A few miles out of Howtown the leaders of the Lakeland 50 race flew past us. The 50 race had started at 12 noon that day from Dalemain which we had passed a few hours earlier. David congratulated the leaders and they wished him well. I knew that for the rest of the race back to Coniston this would now be a common occurrence. Lakeland 50 runners would come past us and hopefully any compliments and support they gave would help keep David going. Boy did he need as much support as possible.

The descent from Wether Hill down to Haweswater was again on the wrong track. I say again because David and I couldn't find the right track the year before, when we were doing the 50. So after two attempts we still have not found the correct sheep trod to follow and most of the other runners hadn't, given the amount of ferns that had been trampled down. David was however prepared for the rough shore line path after last year.

The light drizzle had now turned into persistent rain and more pessimistic thoughts started coming back into David's head. I guessed that in his mind he was thinking of the consequences of quitting. The race was undertaken to raise money for Ashgate Hospice, a local hospice in Chesterfield, and the MS Society. The generous customers and staff at the Pharmacy where David worked had pledged over £1000. By not finishing he would be letting them all down. He also had run a competition to guess his finishing time. What would he do now if he failed to finish? Change it into "Guess my quitting time?" I don't think so. How would Ann cope? She says he's a pain to put up with when he finishes a marathon. If he failed to finish he would be a nightmare to be around. He needed some positive hypnotherapy. It was a shame I wasn't his trigger point for positive thoughts, as he was constantly touching me.

All these thoughts were in David's head when we got to the Mardale Head, checkpoint 10 (75 miles). Considering it was in the middle of nowhere, this was a very good checkpoint, with several food and drink options. The coke helped perk David up, although I think he needed something a bit stronger from the pharmacy. Unfortunately a few chocolate biscuits and a cheese roll would have to do.

Although his mind wanted his body to quit at Mardale Head, David could see no point. It would have taken ages to get back to the finish, either via the organisers or by trying to get a taxi. He would get cold during this time and he had no hot food or drink. He convinced himself that to carry on up Gatescarth Pass was the only option. We were heading to Kentmere, a major checkpoint, which had been excellent last year on the 50. Better to give up there, David thought.

One piece of advice David had been given from a fellow competitor was "Just keep moving and you will finish". As he climbed up Gatescarth Pass the wind strengthened and the rain lashed down. He kept moving forward…just, stabbing me into the ground slowly but surely. Small fairy steps, one after another. He was glad he had invested in the new Gore-Tex jacket. It was just about keeping him warm so he did not have to put any more layers on.

Amazingly few people passed us going up the pass. I guess the others must have been finding the conditions tough. Coming down the other side David cursed every rock and stone on the track. Both his feet were quite painful now, but he was starting to learn to live with the pain and using me more like crutches to soften the impact of every foot strike. Ann, his wife, suffers with MS. She has to put up with pain every day of her life. He only had to manage for a few hours then things would get better. A positive thought at last.

As the rain and wind eased off he was passed by a competitor running the 50 with his dog. These distractions helped to keep him going. Soon we were descending into Kentmere (checkpoint 11- 82miles) and David was so looking forward to a good meal out of the rain. The helpers at the checkpoint were fantastic. They got him a fruit smoothie. This was followed by a dish of rice pudding and then two bowls of pasta, in that order. It all tasted great to him. There's no accounting for his weird tastes. I was left out in the rain while he kept dry.

Kentmere was a mental turning point for David. He knew Ann would be waiting for him at the next checkpoint so there was no way he was dropping out at Kentmere. He was definitely going to get to Ann.

David left Kentmere and for the first time in the race he believed he could finish. His feet were painful but by putting an enormous amount of pressure on me he could combat the pain. He cursed all the rocky terrain. David had cooled down a lot at the last checkpoint so he was grateful of his fleece and even wore his balaclava for a while. He did look like he was going to rob a bank. Thankfully I don't think the fashion police were in the area.

On the approach into Ambleside he followed a 50 runner and together we carried on up Hundreds Road to the waterfall and on to Wansfell. David had missed the sign which would have taken us down to Skelghyll Wood. It cost us about a mile in distance and 30 minutes in time. It was a warning to him to regularly check his Satmap. He did have to "keep going" to finish but he must be "going" in the right direction. The race was tough enough without adding on extensions.

We came into Ambleside (checkpoint 12 – 89 miles) just as the light was failing. David eagerly looked for Ann but strangely she was not there. Little did he know that when he said he would be there for 11 o'clock he had not made it clear that it was 11pm and not 11am. What a plonker.

Poor Ann had waited all day from 11am to 10pm for him. She had gone without food during all this time, just in case she missed him. She finally left at 10pm, tired, frustrated and famished. We had missed her by less than 30 mins. David had tried to ring Ann at Kentmere to give an estimated time of arrival for Ambleside but he could get no signal. His mobile phone had then tried to change networks and then died on him. He had therefore been unable to talk to her since Dalemain. He had loads of excuses but I doubted whether Ann would be so understanding when they finally met. (This mistake cost David a handbag and a pair of earrings).

At Lakes Runner, the checkpoint, David was able get his Camelbak topped up with orange and water. He knew from last year this would be sufficient to get him to the end of the race. He also knew that time was firmly on his side as 2.5mph pace would get him to Coniston before the cut off. He set off, wondering what had happened to Ann. He decided that she must be unwell and back at the B&B but she would want him to continue and not worry about her. He decided it would be best not to contact her until the end of the race, so if she was unwell she could get some rest. I guess there was a little bit of consideration for others in his thoughts.

The route to Langdale (checkpoint 13) seemed totally different in the dark compared to in the light the year before. The 50 runners who came past us were a great help to David, as they were now coming past at a pace we could keep up with for a while. The last group to go past were still at the Langdale checkpoint (95miles) when we arrived. David was determined to go out with them on the next leg as he knew from last year the navigation was a little tricky. The beef stew was excellent at Langdale checkpoint but David had no time for seconds. He had to keep up with the others. I was sure his body weight wouldn't have dropped that much with the amount of food he had stuffed in his face all race. In fact he may well have put on weight, considering the strain he was now putting on me.

We left Langdale with the four 50 runners, as planned. David knew he just had to stay with them and we would be home and dry. It was make or break point. Coniston seemed pretty close, just 10 miles away. When the others walked he could keep up with them easily. However when they ran it was murder to ignore his pain and keep up with them. The alternative of getting lost and having to try and navigate for himself was sufficient to motivate David to keep up with the others. They also gave him loads of encouragement and he felt like royalty, even though they must have been getting pretty tired by now, as well as doing the navigating. He was very grateful for their assistance. I was grateful that at last I had another pair of poles to talk to. We were able to discuss how the race had been for each of us. I think the other poles were in awe of our achievements. I felt 10ft long.

David was relieved when we finally hit the road at the bottom of the Wrynose Pass. He was confident he could navigate from there to Tiberthwaite, the last checkpoint before Coniston, so he let the four 50 runners go ahead. As he looked back he could see a line of lights coming down from Blea Tarn. This train of lights was soon overtaking us, up the last rocky section leading to Tiberthwaite, but David wasn't bothered as he knew he was going to finish. I knew too.

Then something happened that made me question David's sanity. Up ahead he could see a firefighter just standing in the middle of the track. A little strange you would say for 2am in the morning and no fire anywhere near. As David got closer he disappeared. Then David saw a huge rabbit in the distance but again it disappeared as he got closer. I wondered if he had taken something from the pharmacy after all, until I worked out what was happening. David was hallucinating. Many weird and wonderful images came and went in the light of his head torch light before we reached the Tiberthwaite checkpoint. It was a strange but amusing experience for me. I'm not sure what David thought of it but I found out later from other poles that it was a common occurrence. So David wasn't the only lunatic doing this race.

At Tiberthwaite checkpoint we came in just as two 50 runners were leaving so again David decided to go straight out with them. He knew the last 3.5miles to Coniston were not going to stop him, although a set of steps out of the checkpoint car park had a good go. At last he was able to give some navigational help to his new companions. As we climbed up Crook Beck the dawn began to break. I could see lights behind me in the distance. David decided no-one was going to come past him from now until the finish. He also checked his watch and for the first time worked out a possible finish time. We had 1 hour from the top of the col to make it back to Coniston if we were to break 36 hours. We had a target. It was going to be a sprint finish.

It was on the decent from the col that we came across Mark, Catherine and Philip, who we had last seen at Dalemain, half way, when they all looked strong and David was feeling awful. Catherine looked to be in serious pain with every step she took. David tried to offer her encouragement, saying the pain was temporary and it would soon all be over.

David hobbled down the fell-side as quick as he could then he tucked me under his arm and set off towards the miners bridge chasing a different two 50 runners. He caught them at the main track and they ran along together. Then someone mentioned a sprint finish and how foolish it would be to try it, just in case you pulled a muscle so close to the race end. In David's current state of mind he liked this idea, so when the tarmac finally arrived the sprint started. He was oblivious to the pain. As he ran along with me under his arm having a well-deserved rest, I remembered how we had been at the back when we came up this road some 35 hours ago. David ran as fast as he could into Coniston, all the way to the finish with the 50 companions hot on his heels, but his competitiveness was not going to let them pass him. We finished 37th in 35hrs 36mins 4secs. 69 runners beat the 40hr cut off out of 123 starters. David had the biggest smile on his face I had ever seen.

It was great to see the Race Director, Terry Gilpin, at the end and David personally thanked him for a superbly organised event. When he finally plucked up the courage to grin and bare the pain of removing his running shoes, he found he had lost 1.1kg during the race, which apparently was average for 100 runners. I'd lost nothing but I had gained a few scratches along the way. They were battles scars which I was proud to carry.

The pain on removing his running shoes had been so excruciating that David decided not to put them on again. Ann picked us up and was brilliant at attending to David's blistered feet, although he did squeal like a girl. A cold bath certainly helped his aching legs. He was in such agony that the coldness of the water was unnoticeable. David slept till early afternoon with his feet overhanging the bed. He could not bear to have anything touch them. What a wimp. I spent the day in the car boot.

David hobbled around Ambleside that evening and we returned to Chesterfield the following day. He was grateful they had brought Ann's automatic car. The cruise control was a life saver for him. The boot was OK for me, but a little claustrophobic. David saw a chiropodist back at Chesterfield, who sorted out his blistered feet and assured him he and his big toe nail would soon part company. David's right foot turned out to be the worst, the one he had not bothered to attend to during the whole of the race. Yet another mistake he had made.

David hobbled around for about 4 days after the race. He was unable to wear his normal shoes for work and had to resort to a pair of crocks 3 sizes larger. The fashion police were soon on to him. I came away with so many great memories from this tough but most rewarding race. Together as a team David and I had triumphed. I was ready for the next challenge, to show what I could do in helping David achieve his sporting ambitions and raise money for worthy causes along the way. Bring them on.

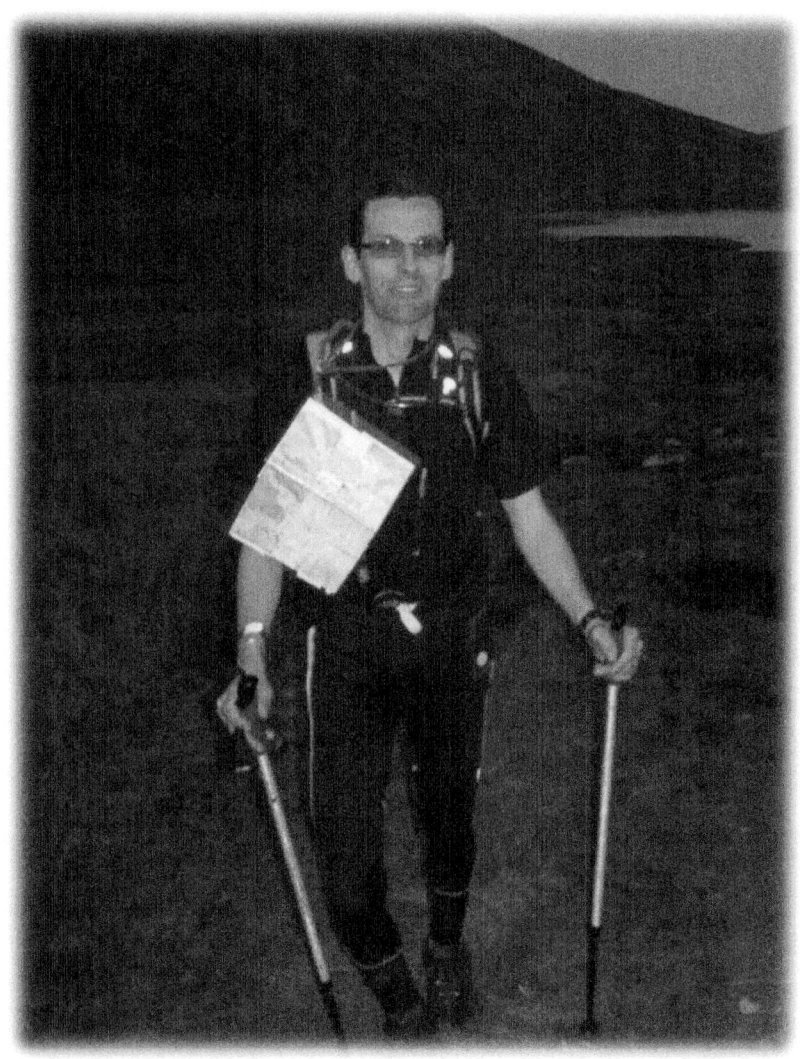

Nearing Checkpoint 3 at Wasdale Head with 19 miles covered, not lost and glowing magnificently.

Chapter 4.

Hadrian's Wall

Don't be afraid of being different. Be afraid of being the same as everyone else – author unknown

My owner, David, would choose one event each year to raise money for charity. The charities he supported are very close to his heart. He started in 2001 raising money for the local hospice in Chesterfield, Ashgate Hospice. He never wanted to do something that everyone else could do, he always wanted to make it that little bit more challenging to catch the attention of potential sponsors. After all, there are literally thousands of people raising money for very worthy charities, so you have to stand out from the crowd.

Ashgate Hospice had cared for his mother in law, Irene, during her last few weeks. The loving care she received was beyond what you would expect. Nothing was too much trouble and no request refused. Irene would never ask for anything. She never wanted to burden others. The care, however, went further than just Irene, and the whole family were accommodated to make this difficult time as easy as possible.

After Irene had passed away David and his wife Ann wanted to do something as a small token of gratitude for the care that Ashgate had given. So the following year he ran the London marathon for them. Nothing special about that, I hear you cry, and you are quite right. That's why he got Ann to make a costume for him and he ran the marathon dressed as Winnie the Pooh. To thank his sponsors he put all their names on his back and carried them around the course.

The following year he managed to get a place in the London marathon and this time ran as Tigger. This carried on every year until his wife Ann was diagnosed with Multiple Sclerosis. He now had a new charity to run for, the MS Society, who had just started up a branch in Chesterfield and were desperate for funds to get up and running. He did not forsake Ashgate Hospice he just split the money raised between the two charities.

The Hadrian's Wall run is advertised by the outdoor events team, Rat Race. They say in their blurb that you have had 2000 years to train for it. It is offered in two formats, either as a single run or as a two stage run with an overnight stop half way. David has always chosen the hardest option in every event he has done. He loves the challenge of putting his body up against the toughest physical challenges he can find. So there was only going to be one option to take, the single stage run, 69 miles nonstop from Carlisle Castle to the Millennium Bridge, on the quayside in Newcastle. This was his challenge for 2013.

Having done 105 miles in the Ultra Tour of the Lake District (Lakeland 100) in 2010, this seemed pretty straight forward. So naturally he had to make it tougher. With a lot of help from Ann and her brilliant sewing skills they put together a Roman Centurion outfit, complete with helmet and tunic. To disguise the ruck sack which was carrying compulsory kit demanded by the organisers, such as first aid kit, waterproofs, compass, emergency blanket, whistle, food, drink etc. they used a long red cape. And on the back of his cape he carried a sign with all his sponsors on it, as was customary.

The problem now was me. As far as I am aware walking poles were not around 2000 years ago, but David did not want to risk injury by undertaking the event without me, his trusty poles. The solution was ingenious. He covered me in cardboard and then tin foil. I was transformed into walking swords – impressive. I did feel a little claustrophobic in my new outfit but at least my tips were out at the bottom of the swords, so I could get stabbed along at David's content. The only problem now was getting the organiser's permission.

Race check-in took place the day before the race at Carlisle Castle. After getting all his compulsory kit checked David sheepishly asked where the organiser was and was directed to a man busily attending to construction of the start line. He politely apologised for interrupting him then went on to explain his intentions to run in fancy dress. He got his mobile phone out to show exactly what the costume consisted of. There was then a long pause while the organiser digested the information. After giving it careful consideration the organiser gave his approval as long as the compulsory kit was carried as per all the other competitors. My time as walking swords had arrived.

David was staying at a hotel in Carlisle city centre. Early the following morning he donned his Roman centurion outfit, grabbed me, the walking swords, and headed out for the 7am start at Carlisle castle. Even though it was less than a mile, I could tell David was very nervous as other runners stared at his outfit. It was certainly getting plenty of attention, as was I.

At the castle entrance he got a couple of marshals to take his picture with me high above his head, glinting in the morning sunlight. I felt great, I think David felt a bit of a Wally. However as soon as we got into the castle grounds we were surrounded by hundreds of ultra-runners, all decked out in the latest kit, looking very serious about the 69 mile journey ahead of them. David could feel all their eyes on him and he just wanted to vanish in thin air. If only Harry Potter invisibility cloaks existed. He found the quietest corner of the courtyard and tried to hide himself away.

As the start time got nearer and the runners started to line up David came out of the shadows and took his place in the field. Not many of his fellow competitors spoke to him, I guess they thought he was a little touched in the head. I did however get some compliments. They were very impressed by the swords idea.

When the start signal sounded we all ran out of the castle grounds, David carefully carrying me so I didn't stab anyone. He was using a run, walk strategy which consisted of 3 minutes running and 1 minute walking. This soon saw him fall to near the back of the field as the rest of the competitors were all running at this stage.

David was confident with his strategy as he knew this would get him home in about 15 hours if he kept it up. He knew even pacing was the key and it was imperative not to go off too fast at the start, as you would pay for this initial over exertion during the latter parts of the race. He also did want to finish in daylight as high vis. clothing and head torches probably weren't around in Roman times. Now a flaming torch would have been ok but there may have been a few health and safety issues to address.

In these early stages some of the other runners thought that David was totally out of his depth and he received a few derogatory comments from runners coming past him. He bit his lip and tried to ignore them. I'm sure he would have liked to have tripped these runners up by holding me out. However, the longer the race went on the more confident he became in his costume and race strategy. After 5 miles he was holding his position and by 10 miles he was overtaking those that had gone off too fast.

At the first check point we were making good progress. David stopped for some food then he was off again, wasting as little time as possible. Unlike other ultra-running events we had done, this one was fully signed so there was little chance of getting lost and David did not have to follow people to keep on the correct route. Normally he would have waited for someone else to have left the checkpoint then followed closely behind them. Now there was no need to employ these sneaky tactics.

Shortly after leaving the first checkpoint the clouds rolled in and the sky began to darken. It wasn't long before the first few spots of rain began to fall and this led to a steady downfall. Me being made mainly of aluminium had no problem, however torrential rain could easily turn my sword costume into a soggy mess which would have totally spoilt the effect.

David had a quandary. He didn't want to get soaking wet as this could jeopardise his chance of finishing particularly if he got cold, then hypothermia could set in. There was also the small problem of his helmet going rusty. He was quite a worrier at times. On the other hand, who had ever heard of a Roman centurion wearing a Gore-Tex waterproof and rain bonnet? What does a fancy dress runner do?

The worrier turned warrior and while those runners stopped to put on waterproofs he bravely carried on, defying the elements. This is what Roman soldiers would have done two millennia ago. There was no time for being a wimp. He stabbed me into the ground more firmly than before and we marched through the rain to the half way point.

By the time we reached half way the rain had stopped and the costume had survived. I still looked impressive as walking swords and David still looked like a centurion and his helmet had not gone rusty. Half way allowed access to a drop bag and also hot food. Unfortunately there was quite a queue for the hot food and, being an impatient type, he was not going to wait around. So, after applying blister plasters and grabbing the food in his drop bag we were on our way again.

We made good progress in the second half of the race passing lots of other runners while only being passed once ourselves. It's great to go past someone and see the look on their face as they realise they are being passed by a fancy dress runner with swords. Everything was going well until we reached the outskirts of the town of Corbridge.

In the distance I could just make out two people in uniform walking towards us. As they came closer I realised they were police officers. Now I'm not sure what they made of David and me. I'm not brilliant in making out human facial expressions, but the officers looked concerned, if not a little fearful. We drew closer and I'm sure one of them was moving his hand a little nearer to his stun gun. This was not a good sign. Electric current goes straight through me. Did you know that I'm the 4th best conductor around behind silver, copper and gold? There is no end to my talents. However, David would have been a poor conductor and a stun gun could have disabled him instantly, as well as ruining his hair.

Thankfully a smile crept over both officers' faces as they realised we were not as it seemed and the tension eased. We had survived the encounter unscathed and the two officers even offered words of encouragement to help us on our way. Nothing was going to stop us now.

After the last checkpoint David decided to run the rest of the route, so I got an easy ride into the finish and could enjoy myself. The light was failing fast and the quayside was just starting to come to life. We got plenty of shouts of encouragement as we neared the Millennium Bridge.

Ann had managed to drive from Carlisle to Newcastle. Not an easy task, as everywhere the Sat. Nav. took her there were road works and diversion signs. In fact she took nearly as long to get to the finish as we did. But she made it and was there, camera at the ready. David held me over his head and sprinted like a demented fool towards her and the finish. I looked resplendent, he looked crazy. Together the Roman centurion and I raced across the line finishing in style and ahead of schedule in 14hrs. 24mins. It was my first and only fancy dress run, and what made it most worthwhile was knowing we had raised over £1500 for Ashgate Hospice and the Chesterfield branch of the MS Society.

My first fancy dress outfit – walking swords. Outside Carlisle Castle ready to run to Newcastle along Hadrian's Wall.

Chapter 5.

Enduroman Double Ironman

If it is important to you, you will find a way, if not you'll find an excuse – author unknown

My owner was always looking for more and more punishing events to push him to his limits and hopefully impress potential sponsors so he could raise more money for his charities. Up to 2014 he had completed 6 ironman triathlons (2.4 mile swim followed by a 112 mile cycle and finishing with a marathon), none of which I had accompanied him on. In 2014 I got my chance.

He was always scanning the Internet for endurance events and he came across Enduroman, who organised multiple ironman triathlons down at Avon Tyrrell in the New Forest, Hampshire. Before his wife and I knew anything about it he had signed up to a double ironman (4.8 mile swim, 232mile cycle and 56.8mile run). I would get my chance to shine in the run if he managed to get that far. It was a big if, as he had never open water swum more than 2.4 miles and his longest ever cycle ride was 180 miles, but that was 20 years ago.

He was soon doing his research to see how much training he needed to do to successfully complete this challenge.

He bought the only book he could find on Ultra Triathlons "Beyond the iron" by Wayne Kurtz, which was filled with loads of useful information as well as incredibly tough training schedules. He read every race report he could find on tri talk and other websites on the Double at Avon Tyrrell, and watched all the You Tube videos he could find. He also contacted Dave Myles, a deca ironman triathlete, for training advice. Preparation was the key to success.

One thing was certain, David knew he had to spend as much time cycling as possible. Dave recommended 600 miles a month, so that was his aim. Bike and I get on pretty well together. I'm sure we are related if you go back sufficient generations. We have many similar features.

David would spend hours and hours with Bike during his triathlon preparations. I started to feel quite forgotten about. Things became even worse when he started buying Bike presents, like fancy new lights. I wasn't jealous, no really I wasn't, because I knew he would need them when cycling in the dark during the event. I just thought he could have bought me something as well. The final straw was when he got Bike serviced. I started to resent Bike after that.

In late February I had to chuckle to myself when David and Bike had a bit of a cycle disaster. David was about 10 miles from home, at 6.30am on a Sunday morning, with the intentions of staying out 8 hours with Bike. It was pitch black, and hurtling down a hill at 25mph Bike hit a large pot hole and suffered a blow out on both tyres. Guess those presents weren't that good after all at lighting the road up.

This caused David a dilemma, as he only had one inner tube. He was forced to ring Ann and like the fantastic wife that she is, she came out in the car to rescue him. When we got home it was still dark, so Ann went back to bed. I thought this is my chance, we can go out and practice with the head torch but no, I was wrong. David got on the turbo trainer in the garage for the next 4 hours. I never got a look in.

At the start of April David put notices up in the Pharmacy where he worked, informing all our customers about what he was planning on doing and asking for sponsorship for the local hospice and the MS Society. He also set up a justgiving website and emailed all his contacts with his intentions. There was certainly no going back now.

He managed to swim the full 4.8 mile distance in March in a pool. In April he did his longest cycle ride of 150 miles and he ran 2 marathons, each in under 3 hours 30 mins. Then just to show he was human and not as reliable like me, he came down with a cold and lost a good 2 weeks of training.

At the start of May David joined the Yorkshire Swimmers at Harthill for some outdoor swim sessions. He has such a puny body that he would cover every part of it with neoprene to ensure he couldn't feel the cold. Personally I'm not a great lover of water, particularly my steel tips, which tend to rust.

Two weeks before the event David finally began to taper his training, which was quite ironic as he had barely picked me up all year. The week before the Double he started to get all his kit together, and there was loads of it. Thankfully he packed the most essential item, me.

We all travelled down to Avon Tyrrell and checked into our accommodation for the next 3 nights, a 6 berth log cabin. It may have had 3 bedrooms but one became the bike clothing and equipment room and the other the run clothing and equipment room, which included me.

David visited the nearest Tesco Express for food supplies. I'm not sure what he was thinking, but he totally over bought. He must have thought he was buying food for an Everest expedition, as he came back with bags laden with coke, Lucozade sport, sausage rolls, Jaffa cakes, scotch eggs, pizza, lasagne ready meals, two ready to eat pasta pots, tinned curry and rice, rice pudding, instant porridge, Weetabix, bread, crisps, mini cheddars, apples, satsumas and a load of bananas. It's a good job walking poles are low maintenance, although love and attention and the odd present would not go amiss.

When David returned from race registration and briefing later that day he looked excited, but nervous. I was glad I was in a separate bedroom that night as he tossed and turned, then at 4am we were all awoken by his alarm going off. He never does getting up quietly. He really should take a leaf out of my book. You'll be lucky to get a squeak out of me.

After managing to force a porridge pot and a couple of slices of toast down him he was off with Bike for the bike check and racking. Bike was very lucky as he got the honour of carrying all 228 sponsors on his aero bars. Why did I never get picked to carry the sponsors? Life was so unfair.

I now had time to chill out and relax, as David needed to complete the swim and cycle before I was called into action.

At 6am the race started with 28 laps of the lake at Avon Tyrrell, which was equivalent to 4.8 miles. Thankfully he didn't drown, although he did do a good impression as he tried to shout his number out after every lap as well as carry on swimming. The sensible triathletes just stopped, said their number and continued on their way. Far too simple for David.

He completed the swim in 2hrs 25mins (6th place) and after a quick photo (so vain) ran in his flip flops the 400 metres up to the change tent.

If you want to see something funny then just watch him trying to get out of his wetsuit and into his bike clothes. It's hilarious and I usually fall over laughing when I see what a hash he makes of it, losing his balance and crashing into things like a drunken fool.

Finally after much faffing around he was off on Bike and my chance to shine was getting a little closer.

From what Bike tells me, the hardest part about the cycle was avoiding road hazards. There was a herd of cows crossing the road at Birley, a group of pony trekkers again crossing the road at Birley and wild ponies wandering free throughout the New Forest with no regard for the Highway Code or other road users.

The next time I saw David was at 7pm when he came back to the log cabin for food. He had covered 13 laps of the 11.6 mile course with 7 laps to go. A 40 min break followed where he devoured curry and rice, followed by chocolate pudding and custard. Then he put his reflective jacket on as dusk was falling, turned on Bike's new lights and continued on lap 14.

By 1pm he was coming in on his last cycle lap, which caught me a little off guard as he was 2 hours ahead of his own schedule and very pleased with the way things were progressing. He had finished the bike section in 16hrs 9mins (11th place, Average Speed 14.35mph). With two disciplines down and one to go, my time had come. David changed into his running gear at the lodge, put his head torch on and grabbed me, his trusty walking poles.

We headed back down to the turning circle to officially start the run. 48 laps of a 1.1 mile course. David had never been around the full run course, only sections of it, so on his first lap he wanted to be sure he kept to the correct route. He was glad that he had me to stop him from tripping. Several athletes did fall and injure themselves on the run, so walking poles, in my unbiased opinion, were a good decision.

The route was mainly off road on an undulating course along rough tracks and through woodland. The organisers had sprayed many of the tree roots on the course orange so they looked like giant carrots, but they could not highlight every obstacle. As far as I could see I was the only set of walking poles out in the middle of the night. On David's second lap, Alan, a fellow competitor, who he had chatted to on the cycle, sped past him and he tried to tag along.

Alan was absolutely flying and David almost fell trying to keep up with him (I saved the day, or rather the night). David let Alan go.

There were quite a few runners out on the course and they all appeared to be motoring along. They made David feel really slow and I think the fatigue built up from the swim and the cycle finally began to hit him. It was 1.20am and his body was saying "Enough is enough, let's call it a day."

I was screaming "Let's get on with it you lazy git." He wasn't listening (to be fair I can't speak) and he decided to get 5 laps completed then go back to the lodge for a rest. I ground those laps out for him, but he felt absolutely awful. I remember Alan saying as he galloped past us, "All you have to do is keep moving forwards". Well there were times when David and I were moving more sideways than forwards. It was very demoralising for David and so embarrassing for me.

After 5 laps we returned to the lodge. Ann was surprised to hear us come in. David collapsed on the bed after setting his alarm for a 20 min break. I'm not sure how long he slept for during those 20 mins but I was raring to go. He reluctantly got up and headed out the door and I jumped for joy that we were in action again.

David always takes his iPod with him on endurance events but usually keeps it as a last resort to perk him up and get him moving. He decided he needed it now, even though he had another 43 laps to go. So he set it to the highest volume and we plodded on into the night. The next lap was OK but again fatigue set in and I could tell he was struggling to keep moving. He had lost the normal firmness which he normally holds my handles with and stabs me into the ground. He was, however, determined to do another 5 before returning to the lodge.

He tried drinking coke to perk himself up but I'm not sure if it helped that much. He also tried an energy shot drink to see if the caffeine would help. To be honest you would have thought he had something a little bit stronger up his sleeve given that he is a pharmacist. The caffeine may have helped for a lap or two but he was soon back to his weary self, just trying to keep moving forwards.

By now it was approx. 4am and David was nearing the end of lap 10 (average 18min/lap). At last it was light enough to not need head torches. David decided to stop at the lodge where Ann was again surprised to see him. She was getting no sleep whatsoever with all these interruptions and I was just as frustrated with all this stopping.

He changed out of his high visibility jacket and stripped off a layer so he felt cold. Hopefully being cold would encourage him to run. He also ate a Tesco pasta pot to see if that would help. Then he was back out with his iPod blaring away. I'm not sure whether it was the fact it was now light, the removal of excess clothing or what he had eaten, but David started to feel a lot better and for once I was being carried and we were running, yes, running and even passing people.

We proceeded to knock out the fastest laps of the run. It was a little muddy underfoot in places and he did lose a shoe in the mud on 2 occasions (he used elastic laces which are great for quick transits but mean your shoe is not quite as tight as it would be with normal laces so can get pulled off in thick mud). Naturally I came to the rescue, helping him to keep his balance while he relocated the lost shoe on his foot. There is no end to my talents. I think the extra cushioning of the soft ground helped to stop any blisters forming. I'm sure if the run had been on Tarmac he would have need the two boxes of blister plasters he had bought just in case.

Having reached 12 laps he was desperate to reach 24 laps, half way. We both knew that would only leave us a marathon to do and that would always be possible to complete. So together we pushed on as hard as we could running all the downhills and flats and just walking the uphills. We were the perfect team working in harmony. Our fastest laps were 14 to 19 where we were even keeping up with the likes of T.C., an Enduroman legend (personally I never liked the chap after he called me 'cheating sticks', but David holds him in high regard) averaging 13mins/lap.

We were both on a massive high and delighted to hit half way. Despite the awful start David and I were now within 26 miles of the finish and we both knew we would finish, it was just a question of when. We carried on running the down hills and the flats and walking the up hills. This strategy was working well and we were keeping our place in the race. At lap 34 (10am) Ann had come back out (not surprised she had a lie in with all the disturbances she had gone through in the night from David having one rest after another) and was supporting us on our way. It was great to hear Ann say we only had another 14 laps to go.

Slowly, lap by lap, David was running less and I was doing more of the work as he walked for longer stretches. Our lap times slowly started creeping upwards towards 20 minutes, but the lap numbers were coming down.

On lap 41 I could tell something wasn't quite right, as David's walking and running style changed. His right knee began to seize up and it became painful to run on it. In hindsight this was probably because he was too eager to get to half way as quickly as possible, rather than trying to set a more even pace. I guess I was a little to blame for this. However I did come to his rescue again, as now I was being used more as a set of crutches to do the final 7 laps.

Finally we made it to the last lap, which in the true tradition of Enduroman events is run in reverse so you can 'High 5' your fellow competitors. As we were travelling relatively slowly compared to the other runners we managed to get congratulated on up to 3 occasions by some competitors on our last circuit. Interestingly there were more of my fellow walking poles out on the course and I felt 10 feet tall as we passed them.

Ann had agreed to meet David at the finish. As he climbed the last hill he threw me to the ground and grabbed the Union Jack flag, which goes with him on all of his major sporting endeavours. I could not believe it, the indignity of it all. Stood up by a flag.

I watched David and the miserable flag disappear into the distance to share the glory moment of finishing, while I just rolled around on the floor. I was totally devastated after all I had done for that man. Where was his gratitude? This was pure pole abuse. If I'd have had the phone number, I would have been straight on to pole line (similar to child line but for walking accessories) and told them about this unforgivable behaviour.

David finished the run in 15 hrs. 00 mins. mainly due to my help. This gave him an overall finishing time of 33 hrs. 35 mins. 05 secs. 10th place overall out of 19 finishers. He may have been a Double Ironman but I was not going to allow him to finish without me again. I had a cunning plan should he decide to try one of these long distance triathlon events again. This did look like a strong possibility given the way he stared in awe the following morning at the athletes who had finished the triple ironman event.

On a positive note he did manage to raise nearly £1500 for his two chosen charities, so I guess some good came out of it.

David struggling to finish the 56 mile run but I got him to the finish.

Chapter 6.

Enduroman Continuous Quintuple Ironman

If you can dream it, you can do it – Walt Disney

The double ironman gave David enormous confidence in his ability to take on challenges which previously he thought impossible. He was ready to try a triple. I had already done a 104 mile run at the Lakeland 100 so a triple ironman, which has a 78 mile run at the end, would present no challenge. Piece of cake.

Enduroman announced the events for 2015. There would be no triple this year, just a quintuple ironman (quin) or a double ironman. Having done the double David did not wish to do it again, so this just left the quin. But was it possible for him to go from a double to Quin?

He emailed Wayne Kurtz, author of "Beyond the Iron", the only book as far as we know about training for ultra-distance triathlons. The answer that came back was a quin was a big step up from the double ironman, especially on the Avon Tyrrell (AT) course. According to Wayne, David would be better to get shorter races under his belt.

I hoped David wouldn't listen to him, as the run on the quin was 132 miles and would be a personal best for me. There was the small matter of a 12 mile swim and 568 mile cycle before getting to the run, but I knew if David could manage these two disciplines I could get him through the run.

First of all David needed approval from Ann, who again would be his support crew for the event. As Ann suffers with MS they really needed a lodge at AT for the event.

Unfortunately all the lodges had gone the same week that Enduroman announced the date of the event.

So that was that. No lodge - no race. David felt relieved, I felt disappointed.

David kept in touch with Dave M. who had given him advice the previous year on how to train for a double ironman. Dave was also hoping to go for the Quin in 2015 but was suffering with injuries. Then out of the blue Dave e-mailed us to say he had taken the decision not to compete at AT. The lodge he had booked was ours if we still wanted it. Thankfully David said yes, the Quin was back on.

David didn't tell anyone apart from his wife, who was not that impressed about spending a week stuck in the New Forest, but would never stop him in his sporting endeavours. He was thinking that if he couldn't swim 12 miles they may be coming home after just one day. No one took my feelings into account, as usual.

The longest David had ever swum was 4.8 miles in open water, or 10 miles in a pool. The furthest he had ever cycled was 232 miles and the furthest he had ever run was 104 miles with me. So this quin was going to be incredibly tough.

David's training began in earnest. His plan was to concentrate on his swimming and cycling and not to worry too much about the run, after all he had me. He knew that if he messed up on the swim or the cycle he might not even get to the run.

During the working week he would leave the house at 6.30am and arrive back after 8 pm. Ann and I were getting bored as all he was doing was swimming, cycling or working, with the odd marathon thrown in. And when he did come home he would go straight into his strength exercises, which consisted of press ups and three core exercises- planking, Russian twists and mountain climbers. Often he would do these in the kitchen as he prepared dinner, using the microwave as a timer. What a nut case. He would even squeeze in the odd plank exercise at work during lunch time while he read his emails. Can you believe it?

My friend Bike really took a hammering during the Easter bank holidays. Saturday at 2pm, after finishing work, David cycled through to 7pm. Then after a rest to cook tea for him & Ann he cycled on from 8pm to midnight. Sunday morning he started cycling again at 4am through to 7am. Then he had an hour's rest for breakfast, as well as taking Chester, his dog, for a walk and driving his step daughter, Nicola, to work. Finally he cycled from 8am to 1pm, completing 225 miles in 24 hours by splitting the day into 4 individual sections. This was exactly how he intended to tackle the quin. "Fairy steps, not giant steps" as Ann would say. Ann and I were still bored.

What little run training he did consisted of roughly 25 miles per week. Virtually all of this was off road but only one 22 mile run / walk with me, his trusty walking poles.

He ran the Chesterfield marathon in September dressed as Mr Bump. Tragically Nicola, his step daughter, had lost her baby, Theo, at 42 weeks the previous year. After this horrific event the whole family became involved with the local SANDS group (Still birth and neonatal death charity). Theo may have been born sleeping but Nicola had no intentions that he would be forgotten. David started doing runs with a bucket collecting for SANDS and dressing in various costumes, the most popular being Mr Bump and Scooby Doo.

In 2015 the London Marathon in April was his longest run. He ran as a whoopee cushion, as you do and took the Guinness world record for the fastest marathon run as a whoopee cushion, in 3hrs 38 mins. He may have been elated but as I wasn't involved again I felt deflated and let down, as if the wind had been knocked out of me.

In his last 10 full training weeks before the Quin David averaged 19.5 hrs of training per week, consisting of 180 miles cycling, 20 miles running and 7 miles swimming. Each week was different as he trained around family and work commitments, including regular visits to his Mum in hospital 70 miles away after she broke her hip, and being moved to another pharmacy at work, which the company had taken over. All obstacles were overcome, but Ann and I were still bored and longing for race day, May 26th, to come.

The final part of his preparation was the race plan. This consisted of breaking every discipline into manageable chunks. The swim would be 5 ironman swims with a nutrition break between each. Swim time was planned for an easy 7 hrs with a 1 hr transition and so on the bike within 8 hrs. The cycle would be an ironman distance (112 miles) on what was left of the first day, then a double ironman distance (224 miles) on the second and third days. The run was then a double marathon on days 4 and 5 leaving a marathon to run on the last day, to finish before the cut off of 4pm. I just hoped he would keep sufficient energy back for the run.

As an extra incentive, to keep him going when the going got tough, he had a notice put in the company weekly newsletter about what he was attempting, and offered a bottle of champagne to everyone who sponsored him if he failed to finish within the 130 hr cut off (he potentially would have to buy 500 bottles if things went wrong). He made notices to go on his running shirts for each marathon on the final run, from 1 to 5, and he dedicated each marathon to those people who meant the most to him; his parents, Ann's parents, his sister's family, his step children's families and Ann. Finally Bike got to carry all his sponsors on the aero bars again like last year for the double ironman.

He took everything and the kitchen sink to AT. He had enough food to feed him and Ann and probably most of Hampshire for a month and all the blister plasters from his pharmacy. As regards clothing and equipment, he had at least two of everything except a wetsuit and me. Yes only one pair of poles were needed, as he had the best and I was going to prove it.

Unfortunately he packed the Union Jack flag, but the flag was not going to get all the glory this time, like he had a year ago at the double ironman.

You could sense David's apprehension when we got to AT. This wasn't helped by mingling with the other competitors, most of which were more experienced than him and Bike felt totally out of place when he saw the multi thousand pound time trial bikes with aero wheels, streamlined drinks bottles and time trial helmets.

Finally race day arrived and David's alarm went off at 4.34am. 4 is his lucky number. He always sets his alarm so he wakes up at a time ending with 4. My lucky number is 2 as I have two of everything.

Trying not to disturb Ann, David had breakfast, smothered Vaseline everywhere on his body, twice, got changed into his swimming gear, kissed Ann and set off to the lake.

On Tuesday 26th May at 6am the continuous Quintuple triathlon began. It was the first time that such an event had ever been staged in the UK and 9 ~~idiots~~ finely tuned athletes set off on a journey which would take both their mind and body to places they had never been before.

David immediately won the competition for most items worn during the swim with three swim hats, a wet suit, two under vests, and booties. He was certainly not going to fail due to cold. In fact failure was not an option. With two years training and £1000 of sponsorship he had to succeed and I needed my chance to show what I was capable of. It wasn't all David, David, David, you know.

The swim was 12 miles. He got into a good rhythm from the start and kept going, reluctant to stop due to fear of getting cold, but knowing he had to eat and drink to keep his strength up. After 5 miles he made his first stop for nutrition, keeping it as brief as possible so as not to waste time. It was cold getting back into the water but it made him swim harder to keep warm.

At his next stop, 7.5 miles, Ann had come down to the lake and she rubbed Vaseline into his neck where the swim hats were rubbing. Two more stops followed for a quick drink and an energy gel. Then with 7 laps to go, according to his counting, he heard the most important words "Last Lap". He finally crawled out of the lake, finishing the 12 mile swim in 6hrs 8mins 02secs, (2nd place). Just the cycle to go then I was up.

The transition from swimming to cycling in triathlon is done by the experts in under one minute. David is no expert. He had a shower and a hot meal before setting out on a 568 mile cycle 30 minutes later.

Then began a routine which was to last over two and a half days. Cycle 5 laps of an 11.6 mile course, then off the bike for a 30min sit down meal and rest. Having come out of the swim

2nd and with cycling being his weaker discipline, David knew it would not be long before the others were catching him and Bike up and overtaking them on their £3000 time trial machines.

He was right, and they came past like missiles, not even giving him or bike a chance to say "Hi". As more and more came past it started to become demoralising but he stuck to his game plan and tried to forget about the others. Thanks to a quicker than expected swim he was ahead of schedule and managed to get 3 extra laps in before midnight.

David's night time routine was to cycle till midnight then start again when it was starting to get light, at 4am. He therefore had 4 hours to sort his kit out, patch up his body, eat and sleep. I think 3 hours sleep was the most he got (he snores so loudly you can definitely tell when he is asleep) but then if Margaret Thatcher could run the country on 4 hours he was sure he could do this event on 3 hours per night.

So into Wednesday we went and the weather was fine, cloudy with sunny periods, but no rain. The cycling missiles were still coming past David, but not quite as frequently. Then Ann gave him an update on his position. He and Bike were still 2nd, but how could that be as everyone seemed to be lapping a lot quicker than them. David decided they must be taking longer breaks and would soon catch up.

The laps kept being knocked off gradually, his back side became sore and he started suffering from neck and shoulder pain. But on he went, even if he couldn't look to either side at road junctions. Some of his fellow triathletes were having even worse problems with saddle soreness and all sorts of padding, including cushions, were being strapped to their saddles to try and improve the level of comfort.

Wednesday's cycling finally came to a close at just before midnight with 21 laps done in the day (243 miles) and now 4 laps up on my schedule.

Thursday dawned and David was back in the saddle at 4am. He was tiring and simple tasks such as getting dressed were taking far longer to accomplish than the previous day. In the early hours of the morning with there being little traffic around David stopped for a comfort break in a small lay-by on the course. As he turned round to get back on the road he totally lost his balance and before he knew it, he was down on the ground rolling around. I think he was more concerned about being seen by a fellow triathlete rather than worrying about any injuries sustained to him or Bike. He was lucky on both fronts, no one saw the incident and he and Bike got up unscathed. Bike did however go on to tell everyone about it. Shame Bike isn't on Facebook.

By lunch David just had 5 laps left. My time to shine was getting close now and I started to psyche myself up and get into the zone. It had been a tense few days for me in the log cabin, getting updates on David's progress from Bike when the pair of them stopped. At 7pm David and Bike finally finished the 568 mile cycle. It had taken them 54hrs 52mins 02secs averaging just over 10mph including all rests and breaks and, amazingly, David was still in 2nd place. He was also 5 hours ahead of his schedule.

Chris Ette, the organiser's son, was surprised when David said he was going straight out on to the run, but I was relieved to be getting going as we had to make full use of the extra time we had, being ahead of schedule. To be honest, I had never expected David to get this far and I was frightfully aware how under trained he was for the run. As the furthest distance he had run this year was 26 miles, 132 miles was going to be well beyond his comfort level and he would need as much help from me as possible. He changed his kit, put his Ashgate Hospice running vest on, grabbed me and off we went.

David's aim was to walk as much of the run as possible and certainly not go off too fast, like he did last year for the double ironman. He was going to start out slow by walking and then in the latter stages, if he felt fit and able, he would pick me up and we would shuffle, or jog, or run. But no running for the first 2 days was the rule.

Out on the course we were the slowest moving around the 1.1 mixed terrain loops. We had to do 120 laps in total so David broke this down into 5 marathons of 24 laps each, which he split into 2 lots of 13 laps.

The objective for Thursday night was to complete 13 laps before midnight. The first lap was just under 20 mins, so we knew this was possible as long as we did not stop long for any breaks.

So our walking journey began. We both were to become acquainted with every tree root, twist and turn of the route. After 10pm it was time for head torches to be worn and we carried on into the night. It was a lovely clear night with the moon shining brightly. I was rather enjoying myself but not as much as David's backside, which was mighty relieved not being anywhere near a saddle. I was urging David to run and I think he was thinking the same, but he kept to the race plan. We walked the 13 laps before retiring for the night just before midnight. Ann let him know he was in third place.

Thursday night was the last night David got undressed before going to bed, after that it became too much of an effort and too time consuming. Lucky for him I'm comfortable being naked all of the time. He was also struggling to sleep due to all his aches and pains and the alarm was getting more difficult to respond to at 3.34am.

However at 4am we were back out on the course walking slowly towards the finish. David had applied plenty of blister plasters to where he thought blisters may form and was vigilant in making sure any sore spots were smothered in blister plasters as soon as possible, to stop anything painful developing. Blisters have never been a problem to me, however my straps have been known to given David blisters so he wore fingerless gloves.

By breakfast, well actually second breakfast as the first one was at 3.45am, we had completed our first marathon. Just 4 to go now. As we started off again we met up with Andy, a fellow triathlete who was trying to complete a triple ironman after his quintuple attempt went wrong in the swim. David loves talking to people when he is competing, as it not only helps him to pass the time and distracts him from his own troubles but you learn what amazing people are competing with you. In Andy's case he was increasing our pace as we stuck to him like glue. Unfortunately Andy was not using poles so I had no one to talk to.

Andy and David walked till lunch, talking all the time. When Andy stopped for lunch David decided to get one more lap in. Half way round the lap the heavens opened and it absolutely threw it down. We kept on going and trudged into our lodge for lunch like a drowned rat. Ann was brilliant at pulling off all David's wet layers as he munched through lunch. But the rain had taken its toll and soon David became very cold. By the time he left the lodge after lunch he was wearing 5 layers as well as a large woolly hat. You would have thought it was midwinter. His Ashgate Hospice running vest was replaced with his SANDS vest. I remained naked.

David was amazingly lucky after lunch to meet up with Ellen. Ellen had done the 12 mile swim on Tuesday, she had then helped with lap counting for the swim in other races which were taking place over the week. She was now running a half marathon. But the best thing about Ellen was she had a pair of walking poles, so at last I had someone to talk to.

Ellen was also faster than us so it lifted our pace nicely. As we all chatted away, the laps slowly disappeared, as did David's multiple layers of clothing as he warmed up. Ellen's poles were great to walk with, telling me about all their adventures in places I had never been to, and all their hopes for the future. They were truly inspiring poles. I was so gripped that I did not have time to worry about my physical state as I was stabbed into the ground every second.

Ellen finished her half marathon and as we continued we started to check out how we were feeling. David's left ankle was becoming sore and at the initial race briefing he was instructed to see the medic as soon as a problem arose, rather than leaving it till it was too late. I had minor metal fatigue but as the organisers had not laid on a metallurgist I would have to grin and bear it.

On David's next lap he went off to see Rich the race medic. Rich looked at his ankle and basically said "What do you expect after everything you have done."

I think David was expecting a little sympathy and a magic cure. He got neither. Rich gave David a few options. Ice it, strap it or use anti-inflammatories. He decided to have it strapped. He didn't want to use any sort of painkiller as he liked to know exactly how much pain he was in and whether it was getting better or worse. I'm not sure if the strapping did him any physical good but psychologically it helped him and, after thanking Rich, we carried on with slightly more spring in our step.

It was not long before David met back up with Andy again and we did a good amount of laps together, but Andy still had no poles, so I was 'billy no mates' again. I did get a little worried when Andy started saying how common psychopathic tendencies are in ultra-distance athletes, especially as we were walking through the forest at night. Luckily I don't think he, or anyone else that night, had such tendencies, as I may have had to be used as a weapon of self-defence, another of my many talents.

Finally it was time to retire for the night. Thanks to the walking companions, Andy and Ellen, we had managed to knock off 47 laps. This was 1 lap down on David's schedule but it meant that we were exactly at half way, with 60 laps done and 60 to go. I was starting to feel confident that David could finish this event, as he had another 2 days to finish. He had a midnight snack before collapsing into bed with an ice pack strapped into his ankle. We were still holding third place.

It was probably David's worst night's sleep. It was too much effort for him to get fully undressed which may not have helped. By the early hours he had exhausted himself tossing and turning. When the three alarms went off at 3.34am 3.40am and 3.44am he slept straight through them. I threw myself on the floor to make a clatter hoping that would wake him, but he was sound asleep.

The next time he opened his eyes it was light and he knew immediately that he had overslept. He got up as quickly as he could, which unfortunately was pretty slow and clumsy.

It was 5:45am by the time the pair of us set off walking. I was livid we had wasted nearly 2 hours but David took a more philosophical view, deciding that he must have needed the sleep.

It was tough for David to get going as his legs were getting stiffer and his feet were sore and painful. I was being used more as crutches to try and make each impact his feet made with the ground as gentle as possible.

After a couple of laps his painful shuffle had increased to more of a walk. Again lady luck was on his side (not mine) and we met up with Andy again, who still had no sticks. He had nearly finished his Triple ironman with less than 20 laps to go, but he was still happy to walk with David. We got into a steady rhythm and again started knocking the laps off.

The two leaders in the Quin, Steve and Douglas, were consistently running past us. They were both heading for a finish today and were certainly in a different league to David. Also going well was Rob. He had initially started out in flip flops but was now in more conventional footwear and eating into our 3rd place. Graham was also hot on the heels of Rob.

Although to finish was everything, David dearly wanted to try and hang on to 3rd place if possible. However with two marathons to go he thought it was still too early to push the pace and start running. For two days we had been the slowest competitor on the run course and things were not about to change yet.

When Andy went for a break Ellen came out to start her final run of the week. She had already done two half marathons and today she was going for 6 more laps. I'm not sure exactly what happened but those 6 laps turned into 13, for which I was very grateful. 13 laps of decent conversation with another pair of poles. We talked about everything from the benefits of cork handles over foam handles and whether compasses were a useful addition to a pole or just a gimmick.

Andy finished his event at lunch time. He looked so fresh but admitted his feet were in pieces. David had lost his two companions. However it was not long before he had recruited two more volunteers to march with him; Graham and Mark. Our group established a 20 minute per lap walking train. I tapped out the rhythm and we strode out together lap by lap. We even contemplated doing the conga as we finished one lap and started another. Mark had struggled with saddle soreness on the bike and was about 25 laps or so behind us but determined to finish. Graham was about 15 laps behind me but catching up fast. Together they shared their experiences of the race so far, both highs and lows.

By late afternoon Steve had nearly finished his Quin. One great aspect about the event was that the final lap for each athlete was done in reverse. This meant you could congratulate each athlete as they were about to finish.

It was not long before Steve was heading towards us on his last lap. Graham and Mark jokingly hatched a plan to push him into the lake while David decided it was just easier to use me to trip him up. In the end David gave Steve a hug of congratulations and Mark and Graham made an arch of honour for him to go under. He deserved the victory having run so hard for the last 2 days. He finally finish in 110 hours, a phenomenal performance and in so doing became the 54th person ever to complete a continuous quintuple ironman in the world, but probably on the hardest course.

Over tea that evening, Ann got the live results up for David to scour over. Douglas was not far off finishing with 5 laps to go, then there were 3 of us with between 30 to 40 laps to go, then

Gary and Mark were another 20 or so laps behind. David was confident of finishing but what position would we come home in? Time would tell. He changed into his final charity running vest, for the MS Society.

After tea David's legs had seized up and it became very difficult to get him going again. He would start out with a shuffle, putting an enormous amount of pressure on me. Even Ann said it was pathetic by her standards and she has Multiple Sclerosis. It took us at least a couple of laps to get into anything resembling a walk. At this stage in the race our time for each lap was going beyond 39 mins.

Just before it got dark Doug finally made it to his final lap and David congratulated him on his achievement as he came past us the opposite way. Doug's 2nd place was even more remarkable when you consider he had no support crew. Sure, others had helped him, but essentially he had been on his own from start to finish. When he had left his cycle lights down in his tent, he had to run and get them. It's all these little things which eat away at your time. I wonder how close Doug would have pushed Steve if he had been fully supported. I think it would have been a close run race.

Back to our race. David really wanted to reach 100 laps before midnight, but according to my calculations at our current pace this looked impossible. Graham had been discussing his race strategy and was planning to go straight through the night without stopping. Rob tended to go for a full night's sleep but then he was running hard all the time and lapping twice as fast as us. He would always say "Hi" as he whizzed past and ask how David was. David would reply that he was going forwards but nowhere near as fast as Rob. It seemed inevitable that Rob would catch us and take 3rd spot.

As it was starting to get dark Steve came back out onto the course to support the rest of us. When he saw David was suffering he shouted, "Get your iPod out." Well, David's iPod is reserved for when he is totally down and out. He finds music to be a powerful motivator. Steve was right, it was time for the iPod. I just wished someone had mentioned it a lot earlier in the day.

Ann helped David put his iPod on. Usually a simple task, but in his zombie like state he was floundering around unable to do straight forward tasks, and was lucky not to garrotte himself with the cable. It's a good job us poles have no cables or switches to worry about.

Finally the music came through the earphones. It was like an electrical charge going into a battery. David picked me up, thanked Ann and we ran off. Yes we actually ran. For three laps I was carried along by David and we were the fastest on the run course, actually overtaking people. TC, the Enduroman legend, described it as Lazarus coming back from the dead. It was a bit of a limping run due to David's painful left ankle but he kept it going around the full laps, up hills as well as down hills.

Mark could not believe it. "What the hell are you doing, that's cheating" he cried. It was fantastic. Best moment of my career as a pair of poles. If only all my brothers and sisters could have seen me. The pain and emotion of this moment had also got to David and he cried, but he did not care.

Slowly the adrenaline began to wear off and after three running laps David did two run / walk laps using me to get him up the hills. By now we had regained the upper hand on both David's schedule and the 3rd place challengers.

We finished the evening walking another three laps with Mark. He had brought his final day total to a manageable amount and we had reduced ours to 19. Under a marathon to go. It was going to be a final day sprint to the line for 3rd place.

David could not afford to oversleep on Sunday morning. It was thankfully going to be the last time we had to get up at 3:34 am. Having slept in most of my clothes it made it a bit easier to get up and out of the lodge by 4am.

His intentions that morning were to carry straight on to the end with no major stops. Again it was tough for him starting off with the overnight stiffness to contend with and he put a lot of pressure on me to help him get going. But eventually his shuffle turned into a walk, even though it was 30 mins per lap.

The first person he met up with was Gary, another Quin competitor. Gary lifted our pace and when he went for breakfast we carried on, half running and half walking, knocking out 20 min laps.

The next person we met was Graham. He had run all through the night and was just 5 laps behind us. Graham looked exhausted but was still going well. He reported that Rob was running fast and closing in on us. So off David and I hobbled, knowing that we just needed to stop either Rob or Graham from lapping us.

Hour after hour went by and we saw neither Graham nor Rob, which meant we were keeping up with them. The laps were coming down slowly, but with each lap completed our confidence grew. When we reached single figures and still had not seen Rob I knew that 3rd place was going to be ours. When David did see Rob he thanked him for pushing him so hard. Without his consistent pacing David would not have upped his pace and his time would have been considerably slower.

The last few laps I planned what David was going to do. Call it Pole hypnotism.

5 Laps to go I got David to wake Ann. Luckily she was already up and highly delighted that he had only 5 laps to go.

3 laps to go and I got David to go around the lap taking as many pictures as he could. I knew he would not do this after he finished but would want a record of what the course was like.

On the penultimate lap I got David to change into his Scooby Doo outfit with the help of Ann.

On the last lap I ran around the course with David and the Union Jack flag stayed in the lodge. David had the biggest smile on his face you could imagine on that last lap. It was a great moment which I will cherish forever, as David carried me aloft and took his time to high 5 everyone, before finally crossing the line 125hrs 12mins and 52secs after starting this event. The run had taken 64hrs 12mins 48secs.

Not only was I the first set of poles to finish but I also became the first set of poles to ever finish a continuous quintuple ironman in the UK. For some strange reason the organisers ignored this fact at the awards presentation the following morning but they did give David a trophy for coming third. Not sure why. For the record Rob came 4th, followed by Graham, then Gary and finally Mark.

More importantly with the help of his generous pharmacy customers and staff we had raised over £1700 for Ashgate

Hospice, the MS Society and SANDS and David hadn't had to buy a single bottle of champagne.

To thank Ann for all her support before and during the event David promised to take her back to her favourite holiday destination, The Maldives, the following year. I assumed he would be taking me as I was crucial to his success, but no I was wrong again. It was to be just him and Ann. How selfish can one get?

The first poles to ever complete a continuous quintuple ironman in the UK with Ann, David and Scooby Doo.

Chapter 7.

<u>The Millennium Way</u>

By failing to prepare, you are preparing to fail – Benjamin Franklin

In 2015 David was trawling through Facebook when an advert popped up for a new event being organised by the company "Beyond Marathon". It was called King Offa's Dyke (KOD) and was a continuous 185 mile run along the Offa's Dyke national trail from Chepstow to Prestatyn. He quite liked the idea, and as it looked as though places would be snapped up quickly, he entered as soon as the event opened. It was a good idea he acted quickly, as all the 100 places were snapped up in hours. I also liked the idea of this event because, unlike triathlons, David needed me for the whole event. Also, if successful, this would be my longest run ever after the quin run.

So with that booked it was just a matter of training for it, and the first event where I was involved was "The Millennium Way". The Millennium Way (6th March 2016) was a 41 mile ultra-run across the county of Staffordshire from Newport in the west to Burton-upon-Trent in the east. The route itself followed disused railways and waterways for most of its length, so has a miserable 300ft of climbing. This was in stark contrast to Offa's Dyke, which has over 29,000 feet of ascent. However, to make things harder, David also booked a marathon the day before, on the 5th March. Unfortunately I wouldn't be needed for that race.

The marathon before the Millennium Way race was called The Groundhog marathon. It was one of these mind numbing track marathons where runners complete 105.5 laps of a 400 metre athletics track. You have to be really stupid to do one of these. This was David's second. Say no more. David was running it as Scooby Doo dressed as a playing card. Boy can he do stupid. I'm so glad he didn't take me. Apart from getting dizzy and totally bored with the scenery, no self-respecting poles would have wanted to have been seen dead with David in such a ridiculous outfit. The lengths these humans go to get a Guinness World Record and raise a bit of money for charity.

Thankfully David took it steady on the track marathon and finished in 3 hrs 42 mins 42 secs and Scooby Doo claimed his first ever Guinness World Record as the fastest marathon dressed as a playing card.

David had covered his feet in blister plasters before the race and everything seemed fine when he finished.

The following day it was my turn in the spotlight. David and I drove to Burton-upon-Trent, the finish point of the Millennium Way. At 7am we boarded a coach and were taken the 41 miles to the start of the run at Newport. As I scanned our fellow competitors I couldn't see one pair of walking poles between them. It looked like I was the only pair. Now, some would say you don't need walking poles for a flat event like this, but this is where they are wrong. I have so many uses that anyone in their right mind would take me.

We arrived at Newport and made ourselves ready for the 8am start. David was running with all the kit he would need for the KOD race later in the year. His rucksack weighed in at 3.3kg. Most competitors were carrying as little as possible, which made us look as though we were intending to camp on route. On the back of David's rucksack he had attached his SANDS sign, complete with a picture of baby Theo's foot prints. He was using every opportunity to raise awareness of SANDS and the great work they do and Theo (David's grandson who was born sleeping in 2014) was here, in spirit, to help us along. Not as though David would need any help as he had me, his trusty walking poles, at the ready.

At 8am approximately 150 runners set off on their way to run the entire width of the county of Staffordshire. David was using a run / walk strategy, which was fine by me. This meant he ran and I was carried for three minutes, then he walked and I worked for a minute. So it was a four minute cycle which was constantly repeated, as we all know he likes the number 4.

The first 12 miles of the route was along an old disused railway track and so was fairly straight. David had done no preparation as regards checking the route out as he was going to try and follow the footpath signs for the Millennium Way, or other competitors. For this first section navigation was easy and we arrived at the first checkpoint with no problems at all.

The next section was a little more complicated as it went through Stafford town centre before picking up the River Sow. David was desperate for a runner to leave this first checkpoint so he could tag on behind but no one seemed willing to leave. I guess the organisers had made the food and drinks available far too appetising or the runners hadn't eaten in days and weren't expecting any more food for the entire race. What seemed like eternity passed until a small group of three runners left the checkpoint and David and I discreetly tagged on behind.

Now I use the word discreetly because normally David bashes me down on the ground as we walk along, sending shock waves through my entire length and sound waves which travel for miles. But not on this occasion. It was as though I had eggs on the end of my steel tips and he did not wish to crush the shells. I was put down on the ground so delicately that no sound was made. David was using devious tactics to secretly follow the runners ahead and hope they did not notice they were being followed. I expected him to dive behind a tree or a hedge if the runners ahead had looked behind.

We headed along the River Sow, through Victoria Park and into Stafford town centre and it was becoming increasingly difficult to try and follow the competitors ahead without them seeing us, but not losing sight of them. After a series of road crossings the runners ahead disappeared into a supermarket car park and were lost from sight.

Great, we were lost. David didn't know if we were even on the correct route. What if these other runners were just after something to buy from the supermarket or had gone in to use the toilets. Sometimes I get so frustrated with my owner. Why can't he just splash out on a Garmin and download the route the organisers gave. Life would be so much simpler. But no, he is far too tight, so we were lost.

We wandered around aimlessly in the car park. I admired the many cars of the shoppers while David worked himself into panic mode. He decided a comfort break was needed out of view of the security cameras, so headed to the far corner of the car park away from the store entrance. Low and behold, on reaching this quiet corner there was a Millennium Way footpath sign pointing us in the right direction. Can you believe his luck? We were back on track.

We were soon onto the Staffordshire and Worcestershire Canal. The canal towpath was again easy to navigate but we had to know when to get off it. The run / walk strategy was working well and although we had been at the back of the field as everyone else raced off, we were now slowly starting to make our way through it. This was a great help as it confirmed to David that he was going the correct way. There is method to his madness of setting off steadily.

At Bridge 105 we crossed over the canal and soon after met two walkers who were half way through a Lands End to John O'Groats walk. It made me wonder whether David and I would ever get to John O Groats. Knowing his navigation he would probably get us lost in the wilds of Scotland.

The only piece of information David had about the route was that we had to leave the canal after Bridge 68. Luckily for him after crossing over Bridge 68, he met up with another runner complete with Garmin and they carried on together.

After leaving the canal the route followed footpaths through low lying farm land. The only problem with such land is that it easily floods and as luck would have it we were about to experience plenty of marshy ground.

Now I don't mind getting wet but David would go out of his way to keep his feet dry. The first bits of marshy ground he used me like a pole vault to project himself over the watery sections. However we soon encountered whole fields which were flooded up to ankle deep in water. The organisers had thrown in a 'Tough Mudder' section and for no extra charge. I enjoyed it but David was not that keen as he squeaked through the water. Flooded field meant I got carried, as if he had used me with his usual force he would have splashed himself, and he certainly didn't want to get any wetter.

After the last checkpoint with about 8 miles to go David forgot the run / walk strategy and ran the rest of the way along the Trent and Mersey Canal and I got a free ride all the way to the finish.

He did however make a total pig's ear of finishing. The organisers had put a big inflatable finish sign up outside the leisure centre, where the finish was inside. David decided to get a picture first before going in to register with the race organisers, so faffed around until he found his mobile phone. He had his picture taken with me, above his head, the first walking poles to complete the route that day, may I add. Then he went inside to officially finish. But instead of going into the room at the entrance of the leisure centre he went straight past and started wandering around the corridors of the centre not having a clue where he was going, and leaving some lovely muddy tracks behind him. Finally, when he had decided he was lost, he asked an attendant, who pointed him in the right direction. We must have wasted 10 minutes, what a disaster. Good job this was just a training run.

We did finally finish in 7hrs 46 mins, 27th out of 119 finishers, and I was the first set of poles. David had covered 67 miles in 2 days and was injury free, thanks to me. What a great start to the year and hopefully we raised some awareness for SANDS.

A horizontal finishing pose at the finish of The Millennium Way.

Chapter 8.

Triathlon X

Difficult roads often lead to beautiful destinations – author unknown

Triathlon X is rated as the world's toughest ironman, with 5137m of climbing. The cycle follows the famous Fred Whitton cycle route, which goes over all the major Lakeland passes, and the run is an out and back route up to the summit of England's highest mountain, Scafell Pike, with over 1400m of ascent . It appeared on Facebook at the backend of 2015 and David got so excited that he entered while the reduced price promotion was on (typical). In his excitement he overlooked the date, 25th June 2016. This is not a date to be forgotten as it is his wife's birthday. He knew immediately he had a lot of grovelling to do.

To make amends David booked the Wateredge Inn, a lovely hotel which is directly on the banks of Lake Windermere, splashing out on a lovely garden room so Chester, their dog, (Bengi had gone to the great kennel in the sky) could come along. Personally I am not a great fan of Chester after he tried to chew me one time, then scent marked me. Me and the flea ridden mongrel with goofy teeth, bad breath and even worse wind are never going to make it as best friends.

After booking the hotel David could relax, safe in the knowledge that Ann would at least have a top notch hotel during her birthday weekend. While he was relaxing safe in this knowledge a deluge of rain hit the Lake District, Lake Windermere flooded and the Wateredge Inn was no long at the water's edge but well into the swollen lake.

Unfortunately the hotel thought they would have everything sorted by June, but they had not, so David got an email two weeks before the triathlon telling him he could no longer stay and his reservation had been cancelled. Being the calm, collected person he is, David then went into blind panic mode and ran round like a headless chicken. When normal behaviour was eventually restored he made loads of frantic phone calls to try and fix up alternative lodgings.

Now David is a great believer that you get as much bad luck in life as you do good luck. Sure enough his luck changed, as there just happened to be a suite left at the Waterhead Hotel, which also borders Lake Windermere but is slightly more elevated. A disaster was averted at the last moment and Ann wouldn't be sleeping in the car at the lakeside car park.

The best thing about Triathlon X was that because the run was so extreme you were allowed walking poles, so I could come along. It would be my first time up Scafell Pike and I was looking forward to being on the highest point in England, with magnificent views all around.

A few years previously David had taken part in the Ben Nevis Triathlon, which was a half ironman triathlon where the run takes you up Ben Nevis, the highest mountain in the UK. Walking poles were allowed but the organisers advised against them due to the number of tourists that would be on the mountain while the race was going on. Surprisingly, and much to my disgust, David actually listened to the organisers and I was left in the hotel room in Fort William while he enjoyed himself. Reaching the top of Ben Nevis would have been the pinnacle of my career, but it was not to be. I think David was hoping to get on the podium and he may well have if I had been there to help him, but he struggled on the descent and missed out on his podium finish. That will teach him not to take me with him. We are a team and there's no I in team.

David, Ann, Chester and me travelled up to the Lake District and checked into the Waterhead Hotel. Chester was pleased as he got his own water bowl and treats provided by the hotel, although he did turn his nose up at the dog bed they provided, as there was already a decent king sized bed in the room for him to sleep on.

I was pleased the Union Jack had not been packed, however David had brought the Chesterfield baby banner. The Chesterfield baby banner lists the names of approximately 200 babies who have been born sleeping or who have died shortly after birth. The babies are referred to as Angels and, as the banner says, it remembers all babies taken too soon. David's intention was to take the banner up to the top of Scafell Pike, with my help obviously, to get them to the highest point in England. He just had to negotiate a swim and a cycle beforehand.

Due to the severity of the course this triathlon started at 4:30am. At this time in the morning there was mist hanging above Lake Windermere, making it look very mysterious. Unfortunately it made it impossible to see where you were going and David does not have the best of eyesight, being very short sighted. To compensate he swims with lenses incorporated into his goggles which were great when they were brand new a few years ago. Now that they are older and show many battle scars from their past the view through them was not that great.

With a combination of early morning mist and scratched goggles he hadn't got a clue where he was supposed to be swimming. He just followed the swim hat ahead of him and prayed that they were going in the right direction. After an hour and 7 mins of swimming somewhere in Lake Windermere he exited the water. He had no idea if he had swum the correct 2.4 mile course but then no one else seemed to know either. Anyway it was one discipline down and on to the bike for 112 miles and 3700m of ascent.

Now Bike had been recently serviced. I have never been serviced in my entire life, not even a clean and polish. Unfortunately David had not properly ridden Bike since that service. He jumped onto Bike and they cycled off through Ambleside, David munching on a banana. It wasn't long before the road headed steeply upwards at the start of the 3 mile (25% gradient) Kirkstone Pass. David changed down into his easiest gear and immediately he knew there was a problem. There was a constant clicking noise.

Now David was no expert on bike mechanics and he knew there was no point in examining Bike as he would not be able to find out the cause of the problem. He just carried on as though everything was fine and arrived at the top of the pass. He didn't need to use the easy gear now until the Honister Pass.

So on David and Bike went, being slowly passed by other faster cyclists. Through Keswick they went and out to Borrowdale and the start of the Honister Pass. He shifted down to the lowest gear and as the gradient increased he pushed harder on the pedals.

All of a sudden there was a loud snap, the pressure on his pedals disappeared and he lost all of his momentum. He then wobbled precariously on the spot, desperately trying to keep his balance, almost bringing down another cyclist and trying to get his cycling shoes out of the cleats. By a minor miracle he managed to avoid falling off like he had done on the quin last year and got a foot out and on to the ground.

He dismounted and checked the damage. The chain had snapped. He certainly did not have a chain tool to mend it and even if he did have the right tool it was doubtful with his limited bike mechanic skills whether he could have fixed it. It was race over, the first DNF (did not finish) of his career was staring him in the face.

David rang the emergency number that the race organiser had supplied in such eventualities but due to the terrain he could not get a signal. He thought about his options carefully. Keswick was about 12 miles away and the nearest place to get bike repairs done. However it would take at least 2 hours to get to running with the bike, by which time the sweep vehicle which followed behind the race to collect stranded and bedraggled cyclists who have not made the cut off times would have picked him up. So he dismissed this option and decided to walk to the top of the Hoister Pass where there was a checkpoint. There may be a solution to his problem at the top, ie a spare bike he could borrow. As if that was likely.

He looked down at the broken chain thinking whether he should take it or leave it. Essentially it was litter and he didn't want to be turning the Lake District into a rubbish tip. However, on the other hand, he did not want to get his hands covered in chain oil which would take forever to remove. Luckily he had put his mobile phone in a plastic bag just in case of rain. So he carefully used the bag to scoop up the chain, trying not to get mucky, and popped the bag into one of his cycle jersey's rear pockets. Then he set off for the summit checkpoint.

As he walked up the road a steady train of fellow triathletes who were still in the race came past him, grunting and groaning as they fought their way upwards. They all thought that David had been unable to handle the gradient so had got off his bike to walk. Quite ironic really, as David is a superb rider when going up hills due to his slim build (he must have a good power to weight ratio). It's just a shame that he is an appalling cyclist on the flat and downhills. David ignored their comments urging him to remount and carry on, smiling politely at them and trying not to let his building frustration show.

On reaching the summit of the Honister pass David checked in with the marshal and explained his situation. He was hoping for some wonderful solution, but the marshal just sympathised with him and said the sweep vehicle would be along in 90 minutes. They were going to be a long 90 minutes.

Then the marshal suggested trying the Youth Hostel which was about 100 metres away. It was probably his last option, so off David ran to see if they could help. When he arrived the warden of the hostel was busily cooking breakfast for the guests. David waited until he had just finished serving a table then timidly told the warden about his predicament and asked if he or any of the guests could help. He shook his head and after asking the guests it became clear that no one was going to be able to offer assistance.

David forlornly made his way back to the marshal at the checkpoint and slumped down next to his bike. He so wanted to get that baby banner to the top of Scafell Pike but how was he going to do it. With him being withdrawn from the race for not completing the cycle section, would the organisers allow him to continue on the run? Or maybe he could get up early and run up and down Scafell Pike tomorrow morning before they set off back home to Chesterfield. He just didn't want to let those Angels and their families down.

While all those thoughts were racing through his head the tail end of the field were still coming up the pass and stopping for water and to catch their breath. Some would ask how David was going on and he would explain his broken chain predicament. They would commiserate with him then would go on their way.

One such cyclist was Peter Smith. He had ground his way up the pass and was now filling up his water bottles ready for the ride ahead. He could see there was a problem and asked David what was up. When David explained the broken chain scenario Peter said he had a chain tool and offered to help. David explained that he would struggle to use the tool due to his poor mechanics, so Peter said he could do it. David then went on to try and persuade Peter not to jeopardise his own race. Peter would lose precious time and he would get covered in chain oil. Peter's response was he needed a rest and he could wipe his hands clean in the grass. Peter was having none of David's excuses. He had an answer for everything. I think he saw this broken chain as a challenge which was not going to beat him. David gave up arguing and the two of them set about fixing the chain.

David was mighty relieved that he had brought the chain with him from the bottom of the pass. Peter examined it and removed the end link saying it was bent and no good. He then joined the end links together, with David offering minimal help, and explained due to the shortened length of the new chain David may not be able to get down to the lowest gear. However a quick trial proved this was not the case, the bike was fixed. David could have hugged and kissed Peter but in the end just lavished him with praise and thanks. Peter went off to the hostel to try and clean his hands off while David continued on his bike, mighty grateful to be still in the race.

Peter was now precariously close to the cut off times when the organisers would pull you out of the race, having wasted 30 minutes helping David. This was something David was acutely aware of. He knew that not only could he not let the Angels of the baby banner down, but he must not let Peter down. He had to finish or Peter's selfless act of kindness would have been for nothing.

With these thoughts in his mind David continued with greater determination than ever. He pushed Bike hard, giving maximum effort the whole way. Failure was not an option now. He fought up all the passes and prayed that God would look after him on the perilously dangerous descents.

Slowly David started passing other riders as he made his way through the field. Even a heavy downpour did not dampen his desire to finish.

8 hrs 58 mins after starting the cycle David came into the transition area. While he changed into his running shoes Bike filled me in with what had happened out on the course. The pressure was on me to deliver and get David up Scafell Pike, complete with baby banner. I relished the pressure and psyched myself up for a monumental effort.

David grabbed me and we charged out of transition. He briefly paused to kiss Ann, who thanked him for the birthday flowers and cake he had arranged to be delivered to their hotel room, then he continued on his way.

His rucksack was so much bulkier and heavier than everyone else's as he had the baby banner as well as the organiser's essential kit in it. But he was not going to use that as an excuse. The extra weight acted as a constant reminder of what he was doing.

His tactics were simple, run the flats and downhills where possible and walk the up hills. This meant for the first 8 miles I got an easy ride. After the downpour on the bike the sun had come out and we were being treated to glorious weather. Using minor roads and tracks we made our way from Windermere through the Skelwith Bridge, Elterwater and Great Langdale to the Dungeon Ghyll Hotel. This acted as a checkpoint where you had access to a drop bag. Many competitors had chosen to pick up their walking poles from here, but not David, we were using teamwork from start to finish.

From Dungeon Ghyll the run route hit the Lakeland fells and I started to work. We slogged our way up to Rosett Pike. The weather was still holding and the views were stunning. I just couldn't wait to get to the top. We were being passed by the leaders now, dancing their way down the mountain to the finish. I wonder how many of them were carrying a baby banner?

On we went past Angle Tarn to Esk Hause where there was a marshal station for emergency first aid.

As we continued upwards the skies began to darken, the wind picked up and I knew rain would soon be on its way. Usually David has his waterproof on well before it starts to rain, I don't think he likes to get his hair wet, but not on this occasion. He wanted to waste as little time as possible. The first spots of rain started to fall and we ignored them and carried on.

The spots soon turned into another torrential downpour, but still we carried on. I think David was trying to get us past the boulder strewn section of the route you hit as you go between Broad Crag and Ill Crag, but we were about 15 minutes too late. The jumble of jagged rocks were soaking wet when we got there. In the dry this section can be a lot of fun jumping from one boulder to another. Now that they had become slippery it looked a dangerous place to be, one mistake could have disastrous consequences. I tried my best to help but just could not get a grip. In the end it was up to David's balancing skills to get us through.

As our pace had slowed at the boulder field David was starting to cool down dramatically, as the rain soaked his cycle top and shorts. Things were not going too well and with mist coming down visibility was reducing drastically.

Little by little we made our way through the minefield of jagged rocks, David managing to balance precariously on each rock and not lose his footing.

In the distance we could hear a bell tinkling. We were getting closer to this intriguing sound, perplexed as to what it could be. We descended off the boulders and there at the bottom of the final climb to Scafell Pike was a marshal ringing a bell. It made perfect sense as visibility was down to about 10 metres.

We passed the marshal and made our way up the last part of the climb. I gave David as much help as possible as I could feel him shaking from the cold, but he was determined not to stop until the summit. Finally the summit did appear out of the gloom and there was a marshal there to greet us.

The first thing David did was to throw me to the ground. This was not what I was expecting. I had dreamed about this day, being on the highest point in England with magnificent views all around. The reality was, I was in the middle of a howling storm on a mountain top covered in mist with no views whatsoever. Great.

David put on his waterproof top. He pulled the baby banner out of his rucksack, rolled out all 6ft of it (The banner is like a plastic groundsheet 6ft by 3ft) The marshal was quite bemused. He couldn't remember that being in the essential equipment list. David explained what the banner represented and the marshal took several pictures for David. I did my best to try and just get into the pictures. I think I made the edge of one.

Then the baby banner was rolled back up and stuffed into David's rucksack ready for our run back to Windermere. We marched off back in the direction of the tinkling bell, knowing we had done our duty and got the Angels to the top of England. David had rather a large smile on his wet face, even though he was uncontrollably shaking from the cold.

It had been hard enough to cross the boulder strewn section on the way up, but it was now twice as difficult, as David's shivering was not helping his balance. Again I was not helping matters as I could not get a grip and David was having to carry me. I could sense his frustration. At one point he was almost on all fours as he literally crawled off Broad Crag towards Esk Hause.

As Esk Hause came into view the rain began to ease and the wind died down. David was beginning to warm up and we were starting to make good progress. A little further on, as we headed towards Angle Tarn, David spied Peter on his way up, chatting with another competitor. David stopped and thanked Peter for about the hundredth time and wished him well for the rest of the run. He knew Peter was very close to the cut off times and any of the marshals could have stopped him and forced him to come down the mountain without reaching the summit.

David and I marched down the mountain and by the time we were back at Rossett Pike, the weather had totally changed and we had glorious afternoon sun.

We negotiated the path down by the side of Ross Gill and as soon as we hit the Cumbria Way, David lifted me up and we ran into the checkpoint at the Dungeon Ghyll Hotel. It was a short stop to waste as little time as possible, just a swig of coke and a banana. Then up I was picked and David charged towards the finish.

Those last 8 miles we flew, never stopping and never walking. David took his mind off any discomfort he was feeling by going through the events of the day. He'd had an amazing day, from the misty swim in the lake to the broken chain and Peter the saviour and finally getting the baby banner up to the summit. I reflected on my day. I, unlike most of the poles, had done the full route. I had joined an elite club of poles that had completed an ironman, a double ironman and a quintuple ironman. What a day.

David and I ran into Watershead just as the light was failing. David had wanted to finish in the light and he had just about managed it. Ann and Chester were there to greet us, although I kept my distance from Chester. We sprinted across the line to finish the run in 7 hrs 33 mins, giving an overall time of 17 hrs 53 mins (56th out of 148 finishers).

As for Peter, well the organisers had set a 20 hour time limit. He finished in 19 hours and 52 minutes, which considering the last third of the run would have been in darkness, was a brilliant time. As far as David was concerned, Peter was the hero of the day.

Top of Scafell Pike with the Chesterfield SANDS baby banner.
Just managed to sneak into the picture.

Chapter 9.

The Yorkshire 3 Peaks for SANDS

There is no foot too small that it cannot leave an imprint on this world – author unknown

Since David's involvement with the Chesterfield SANDS group they have organised a yearly physical challenge for their supporters. In 2015 it was an 85 mile cycle ride from Hardwick Hall, near Chesterfield, to Skegness. That year David took part dressed as Scooby Doo: What a show off. It certainly drew attention to the group and helped raise awareness of the charity. I wasn't involved and had to stay at home and sulk.

A year later and a different challenge was planned. Even better, I would be coming along. Several in the group had expressed a wish to climb a mountain and in response an expedition to climb the Yorkshire Peaks of Pen-y-ghent, Whernside and Ingleborough was arranged.

David's wife, Ann, would dearly have liked to have taken part, but she knew with her MS she would not be able to keep up with the group. So David and Ann arranged several outings to climb each peak separately. The annoying thing was Chester the dog went but I got left at home. There was a feeble excuse that David couldn't handle a dog as well as poles. Well surely the answer was simple, leave Chester and take me instead.

It was not to be and while I was left at home they climbed each Peak in glorious weather. Every time they got into the Yorkshire Dales the sun would shine and at the top of each

Peak the views were breathtaking. David knew the SANDS walkers were going to love their expedition later that year.

A briefing meeting was held a month before, when a kit list was given to each participant. The walkers were going to be led by a professional team who would ensure they got round safely. On their kit list was walking poles, which was brilliant news for me. Not only would I be going along but I would have some company as well. A day of decent conversation was on the cards. Roll on Saturday July 16th 2016.

On the day of the event David was up early, well early for most of us. He was picking up Nicola, his step daughter and then Louisa, a close friend of Nicola's. Nicola and Louisa knew one another for all the wrong reasons. They were both pregnant at the same time and sadly both went on to give birth to sleeping babies. They both called their Angels Theo. One had the surname of Chaplen and the other Chapman. They were both to meet later at a SANDS event when all these coincidences came to light. A good friendship evolved from these tragic circumstances. The coincidences continued as both went on to have a second child. Louisa had baby Ethan in 2015 and Nicola had baby Jenson in 2016.

David had to ring Nicola to wake her up and by 4.15 they were on their way to pick Louisa up, with me packed in the boot with the rest of David's kit. Louisa was ready when they arrived, so they lost no more time and were on their way up the M1. Everything was going fine until the Highway Agency decided to shut the junction of the motorway they needed. Luckily Louisa knew the area better than the Sat. Nav. and she managed to get them back on route despite a few minor Highway Code infringements by David.

As they drove to the 3 Peaks they all witnessed a vibrant sun rise above the horizon, but the nearer they got to Horton-in-

Ribblesdale, where the walk began, the heavier the cloud cover became. It was not going to be such a great day weather wise. Well at least waterproofs were on the kit list, so everyone would have those.

We all arrived just after 6.30am ready for the pre-arranged start time of 7am. The rest of the walkers were arriving and everyone got ready for the start with their wet weather gear at the ready, as rain was imminent. The official guides for the walk had also arrived and they mingled with the group, casually looking at people's clothes and asking if they were actually waterproof.

Things then started to get a little embarrassing for me. David changed into his attire for the event. Not a single piece of Gore-Tex was involved. He donned his Scooby Doo outfit, complete with SANDS vest over the top. As inclement weather was expected he added a rain bonnet (purchased from his pharmacy) and a £1 transparent plastic poncho so you could still see the SANDS vest underneath. He then grabbed me and his ruck sack containing the baby banner and was ready to join the group. If nothing else he was sure to draw awareness for SANDS.

The professional guides were a little taken aback by this outrageous outfit. I don't think they had ever come across such a sight before. A Scooby Doo suit was definitely not on their suggested kit list. There they were, nit-picking at the other walker's clothes when a fancy dress walker joined the group. David was too modest to mention that Scooby Doo had already run four marathons five half marathons and a Guinness World Record that year. He also never mentioned that he was running another half marathon the following day. He just told the guides he knew what he was doing and they should concentrate on the rest of the group instead.

Each person in the group was there for their own particular reasons. Some were walking to remember their own Angels, some were there to support their Angel family friends. Even though the level of fitness within the group varied considerably everyone was determined to do their best for their Angel, whether that meant climbing one, two or all three peaks. There would be no winners or losers today, it was all about taking part, remembering those that were taken too soon and raising awareness for SANDS.

Off the group set at 7.30 due to a few late comers. As there were many different groups also walking the 3 peaks that day the guides made a good decision to do the route in reverse, so Ingleborough at 723m was going to be the first peak. I was loving the fact there were loads of fellow poles around for me to talk to. I hadn't had this much fun in ages. In fact I was enjoying myself so much that I had missed the fact it had started to rain and the higher we climbed the mistier it became, until visibility was severely reduced. In fact on reaching the summit plateau you could not see further than 20 metres.

David stopped at the summit shelter and got the baby banner. Then, with the help of Claire and Jay, they unfurled it and a picture was taken. By now the weather was pretty poor and I think David was regretting his choice of outfit as Scooby was suffering from a soggy bottom.

On the descent David tried to get a few pictures of the walkers. In trying to keep his mobile phone as dry as possible in the now driving rain, he did not close his bum bag correctly and accidentally dropped a bag containing his credit card and £40 in cash. I tried to alert him by falling over in style (it's a shame I can't shout, but I have no mouth), but he carried on regardless. By the time he realised his mistake we were already at the bottom of Ingleborough.

David was none too pleased when he realised his faux-pas. I could tell by the way his grip tightened on my cork handles, as though he was trying to squeeze all the life out of me. I was glad when he let go his strangulation grip and rested at the support vehicles, who were doing an excellent job following the walkers with food and water and supplementary kit.

By the time the ascent of Whernside commenced a few walkers had retired for one reason or another, conveniently at a pub, and the rest of the walkers had split into three groups. David and I were in the rear group.

The weather had improved a little by now with the rain temporarily ceasing. The group slogged up the footpath highway to the summit while a steady stream of walkers also doing the 3 peaks descended. The ascent was tough for some in the group and progress was slow.

At one point David and Drew offered to take a fellow SANDS walker back down the mountain for safety reasons, but the guide declined. He wanted to keep the group together. Again I think he totally underestimated the abilities of David and Drew (Drew had military training and where David was a gazelle, Drew was an Ox, in my opinion). I took the opportunity to chin wag with some other poles.

Finally the summit was reached and this time Drew helped David unfurl the baby banner and a picture was taken. David also had a considerable length of bunting. On the bunting Angel families had written messages about their Angels. David had been reluctant to get the bunting out on Ingleborough as he was unsure just how waterproof each message was, but now conditions were dryer he got the bunting out. Unfortunately the wind was still pretty gusty and he and Louisa struggled to hold on to the many metres of bunting as it flapped about ferociously in the wind. They did however get a picture taken for the Angel families and somehow the bunting was tamed back into the rucksack for the final peak.

Our group finally started the slow trudge back down and past the magnificent Ribblehead viaduct majestically carrying the Settle to Carlisle railway line 400m across the valley. But time was ticking by and David was aware that at their current speed the group would struggle to make the final peak of Pen-y-ghent in daylight.

David asked around and it was clear that about half the group wanted to continue and the rest were happy to call it a day and maybe return at a later date to finish off the challenge. Given that the smaller group would now make faster progress David was confident there was ample time to finish off the walk in day light.

The guide had other ideas. In fact the guide had just one idea and that was to stop the walk right there and then when they reached the road at the bottom of Whernside. Many were surprised and disappointed but being the polite people they were, accepted the decision.

David was having none of it, he can be stubborn when he wants. He had been put in charge of getting the baby banner and bunting to the top of the Yorkshire Peaks. He hadn't failed in a challenge yet and he wasn't going to start now. He politely, but firmly, told the guide he would be continuing. He asked around to see if anyone would like to come but got no takers. Not surprising really, as he had no idea of the actual route to Pen-y-ghent and after a professional guide has said not to continue, are you really going to listen to some plonker dressed as Scooby Doo?

We were on our own, just David and me. We knew there were two groups ahead of us and we knew the route from the base of Pen-y-ghent to the top and that was it. We had no idea where the route went for the next 6 miles to get to the base of Pen-y-ghent.

Luckily Chris, who was a support vehicle driver, told David where the other two groups had gone. I was grabbed by David, thrust under his shoulder and he bombed off in the right direction. We were taking no prisoners now. We were on a mission to get these Angels to the top of Pen-y-ghent and nothing was going to stop us.

The next section of the route was along a country lane. Luckily there were still other walkers on the route, although most were heading in the opposite direction to us so we could not follow them. However we could ask them directions and David found where the route left the road.

We carried on cross country passing two groups who were also heading towards Pen-y-ghent. David asked if they had seen the SANDS group, but they hadn't. They invited us to join them which would have made route finding a doddle but David was keen to catch the other two SANDS groups up.

On we ran taking what seemed to be the obvious route, until we came to a gated road which led past a farm. I was sure we had gone wrong somewhere and David was also getting second thoughts. He tried to consult google maps but could not get a signal and he hadn't bought any paper maps as the walk was being led by 'professional' guides.

As luck would have it he noticed an old lady at the window of the farm house starring at him. How rude, he thought, until his tiny brain kicked into gear and he realised he was wearing a Scooby Doo suit, complete with rain bonnet and poncho, which may have looked a trifle out of place. Well at least he had the ladies attention.

He then tried to ask her the way by using mime, yes mime. "Which way" was acted out by pointing in different directions, "3" was shown by holding three fingers up (good job it wasn't the Yorkshire 2 Peaks challenges) and "Peaks" was illustrated by using me to draw 3 mountain peaks in the air. Amazingly the lady had no idea what David was trying to do and probably thought he had escaped from a local secure institution. She hurriedly moved away from the window, probably heading for the phone to ring the police about the escaped lunatic.

David was getting a little exasperated by now. Why didn't the lady understand his charades skills? I was dying from laughter and embarrassment at the same time. If I could have put this on YouTube it would have gone viral instantly. David decided to carry on for another half mile, then having seen no other walkers in the vicinity we backtracked to the farm.

Luckily the police had not arrived yet, but further up the hill was a farmer on a quad bike. It was our chance to get back on route and we sprinted off in pursuit of the quad bike.
A rather breathless David managed to ask the way for the 3 Peaks and the farmer didn't bat an eyelid at his ridiculous costume as he pointed us in the right direction. He had saved the day and after thanking him we carried on.

It wasn't long before we were passing the two groups which we had already passed half an hour ago. We would have been quicker if we had just stayed with them. If we hadn't have been so distinctively dressed we may have got away with losing our way, but they knew we had gone wrong so we quickly hurried past them before they could laugh in our faces.

The route from then on became a little easier to follow and before long we were approaching the slopes of Pen-y-ghent. David knew this area now from his walks with Ann earlier in the year. The walks where I was left at home in place of Chester the dog.

In the distance, roughly half way up he could make out two small groups of walkers. He decided these must be the two SANDS groups and he calculated that he could catch the leading group before they got to the top. That was his competitive side coming out again. So with no time to rest we were off running again. We had run continuously from having left the 'professional' guide, unfortunately not always going in the right direction (a minor point I'm sure you'll agree).

David and I soon caught the first group containing Julie and Jay, Becki and Rob and their guide. David explained how the last SANDS group which he had been in was stopped by the guide, so he was the only survivor. We then headed off to catch the leading SANDS group, which we did near the summit. Again David repeated the story of how he was the sole survivor of the last group then he shot off to get to the summit first.

Now you may think he was showing off by doing this, but I can assure you this was not the case, as I was there. He wanted to set the summit up for the arrival of the others. On reaching the trig point he pulled the bunting out of his rucksack, together with the baby banner. He then proceeded to wrap the bunting around the trig point. Yes, he used the Angels to decorate the top of Pen-y-ghent. It's a shame he didn't think to do this earlier for the other two Peaks. That was always his problem, he didn't think. Both Ann and I agreed on that.

When the other walkers arrived and again it was a struggle for some as they were pushing themselves to their limits but determined to succeed, they were greeted with the bunting fluttering in the breeze. David and I were rather proud of ourselves. Mission accomplished. The Angels had climbed the Yorkshire 3 Peaks.

The two groups both successfully finished the challenge and, although outside the 12 hour limit normally aimed for, they all seemed proud of what they had achieved. And what made the day more special were the walkers who stayed behind after completing their 1 or 2 peaks to welcome us back. I'll always remember walking down Horton-in-Ribblesdale being held aloft by David surrounded by the SANDS walkers of Andy & Dominic, Chris, Steven and Claire, although only Claire had poles for me to talk to.

David never did get his money or credit card back, although there were rumours of a sheep wearing Vivienne Westwood earrings and carrying a Gucci handbag. Scooby Doo had such a soggy bottom that he was unable to run the Rugby half Marathon the following day so Mr Bump took his place.

A few weeks later Drew, Nicky and her sister returned to the Dales as they had unfinished business to attend to, having climbed two Peaks first time around. Drew led them round and Ann and David acted as support. Good job David did take Ann along, although he left me behind, I hasten to add. He managed to lose his mobile phone and the car keys. The phone was handed in to the café at Horton and Ann found his keys. He has since vowed never to return to the 3 Peaks. Who knows what he will lose next time? His mind?

Talking with other poles on the summit of Whernside while David messes about with baby bunting.

Chapter 10.

King Offa's Dyke

Do or do not. There is no try. - Yoda

David's training for 2016 all centred on the King Offa's Dyke race. By the time we got to the end of September 2016 he had already notched up 2 ultra runs and 8 marathons. In August he had also run 34 miles of the actual route with me and all his kit, from Chirk Castle (checkpoint 8) to Bodfari (checkpoint 10), so we both knew what to expect. We had however become hopelessly lost on the way to the Bodfari checkpoint, but hopefully this wouldn't happen on the actual event.

The race itself was a 185 mile traverse of the English Welsh border, starting at Chepstow in the south and finishing at Prestatyn in the north. Competitors had 96 hours to complete their journey. Along the way there were ten intermediate checkpoints where food and drinks were available as well as the opportunity to rest, if you had sufficient time to. Three of the checkpoints at 50, 100 and 150 miles were classed as major checkpoints where you had access to a drop bag. It was therefore up to each competitor to work out their own strategy regarding resting and sleeping.

David has a liking for these longer events as they test not only your body but your mind as well. You have to be mentally strong because at some time in the race you will experience thoughts of doubt and despair. You will question whether you are able finish. You can be the fittest person going but if you're not prepared for the mind games and how to cope with them, there is a fair chance you will not finish. David is pretty mindless which is why he does so well.

In mid-August David put out his sponsorship forms in the pharmacy, set up a justgiving.com page to take pledges on the internet and basically told as many people as possible what he was attempting to do. Attempting is the correct word to use here because, although he was confident of his abilities, the 185 miles from Chepstow to Prestatyn was still 50 miles further than we had run before and this time he would be carrying a rucksack. He would also have no outside help i.e. friends and family to support him as it would have been difficult for Ann to have tried to follow him in the car. The other big factor was the 9085m of elevation involved in the race, which was more than climbing Mount Everest.

He still offered a bottle of champagne to work colleagues should he not be successful, in an attempt to get them to sponsor him. As was tradition he was going to carry all his sponsors with him, as he was proud they had taken the time to dig into their pockets and support the charities which were close to his heart. But how would he carry them? In the past he had put them on his rucksack, but this time he had a far better idea. He decided he would put the sponsor's names on me, just below my handles. That way he would be constantly reminded of why he was doing this challenge and should he ever get any moments of doubt as to whether he could finish or not, he would just need to glance down at me and see the names.

Being ever resourceful at trying new ways to raise money for his charities he hit upon another brilliant idea. The past two events I had been involved in we had carried the Chesterfield SANDS baby banner up and down mountains. David thought he could use one pole for the pharmacy sponsors and one for Angels. If anyone wanted to let their Angel accompany him on this event they could make a pledge. He wasn't bothered how much they pledged. In return, he would put their Angels name on my other side. He needed to sit down and rest after this idea.

He emailed Nicky, the chair and founder of Chesterfield SANDS, with his idea and asked her to put a post out on their Facebook site two weeks before race day. Nicky readily agreed and posted a message.

David's brilliant idea didn't look that brilliant to begin with. Obviously his own grandson Theo would be on the poles, born sleeping on 1st September 2014, but only one other person replied, Carmen, who asked for her Angel, Grace, to accompany him.

After a week, David asked Nicky to repost on Facebook and this time the response was significantly better. Names started to come in along with very touching messages of gratitude. David would type up the names received so far, waterproof them with sellotape and stick them on to me. Then he would take my picture and repost it on Facebook so the Angel families could see their Angel. I felt so proud to carry these names, especially when you heard the parents' heart-breaking stories. I also felt a huge responsibility to look after these Angels and keep them safe.

The names continued to come in and more of me became covered with the precious names of babies taken too soon. David was struggling to keep up with all the messages containing names. Even on the morning he was due to leave home for Chepstow, he was still adding names to me. We eventually left David's house in Chesterfield with 208 pharmacy customers on my one side and 63 Angels on my other side.

David was going to travel down to the start by train. Simple enough, Chesterfield to Birmingham New Street, then in to

Chepstow to arrive early afternoon, in time for the early race registration. East Midlands' trains had other ideas and when they arrived at Chesterfield station we were greeted with the news that our train to Birmingham was running 70 mins late.

Great. David started to go into panic mode and in so doing managed to lose his debit card. It was a good job Ann was there to take charge and calm things down. The late train meant David had sufficient time to return home, cancel his debit card, transfer money into his joint account and pick up the debit card for this account. What a drama and we hadn't even started the race.

Finally the late train arrived but by now the connections were no longer available. We had to make an additional change at Gloucester so arrived in Chepstow too late for early registration. We would now have to register at the race venue on the other side of the river.

David decided to try and relax, so he went into a local café. Having located where the electrical sockets were so he could charge his phone, he ordered a drink and a muffin then checked his emails. Another three names had come through while he had been travelling. He was prepared for this eventuality having brought a sticky label with him. The Angels Ryan Aaron, William Roy and Ashley were added to me. I now had 66 Angels to carry. With all Angels accounted for we set off for race registration.

The organisers had hired a leisure centre sports hall and there were lots of other runners milling around when we arrived. David marvelled at all the fancy kit they had while I eyed up the other poles that were around.

The organisers were very thorough in checking that everyone had all the mandatory kit. One item had caused David considerable concern; the sleeping bag. He didn't want to carry anything that was particularly heavy as this could jeopardise his chances of finishing. However being a tight so and so, he didn't want to splash out over a £100 on a top of the range lightweight bag which he knew he would be unlikely to use again. Ann tried to come to the rescue by cutting up an old sleeping bag and making it as small as possible. But this wasn't good enough. To get the weight down David wanted to reduce the size of the bag even further. I would have only just fitted in, if Ann had listened to him but sensibly she refused to make it smaller.

So David's next idea was to see if a sleeping bag liner would be acceptable. He emailed the main organiser who agreed, but pointed out that it may not be warm enough. Well David reckoned he'd just put on extra clothing and if he wasn't tired enough to fall asleep straight away then he should be carrying on to the next checkpoint. I could tell this was going to be a very tough event indeed. I would be pushed, or rather stabbed, to my limits.

We successfully got through the kit check and David left his three drop bags for collection during the race. In these bags he had packed clean clothes, food and drink, ice packs, a load of spare batteries and literally hundreds of blister plasters. Compeed profits must have been up that month. In the 100 mile drop bag he put a pair of running shoes one size larger than the pair he was starting with. This was to allow for his feet swelling as the race progressed.

At race registration the organisers gave everyone a tracker device so our progress could be checked. This meant they could see if we were going off course or trying to cheat and take a short cut. I think the former was going to be most likely in David's case. They also gave each competitor a replica coin from the time of King Offa. This was to be carried to the end where it would be exchanged for a finish line momentum, whatever that might be. Should you fail to finish then you got to keep the coin as a constant reminder there was unfinished business to attend to.

Although the race was due to start at 8pm outside the leisure centre and not at the start of the Offa's Dyke walking trail, the organisers wanted everyone to do the whole of the official trail. The first mile of the official trail was quite narrow, so they had decided against using this as the starting point of the race to avoid runner congestion. Instead they walked everyone to the cliffs at Sedbury, overlooking the Bristol Channel and the Severn road bridge in the distance.

David got his picture at the official starting plaque with me and my Pole Angels taking pride of place on the photo. He wanted to keep sending updates back of his progress so the Angel families could see how he was getting on. There was also the tracker which allowed anyone to log in and see exactly where he was. We may have been unaccompanied, but the whole world could have been watching us.

The start of King Offa's Dyke. Just 185 miles to go with 70 Angels to carry and all my sponsors.

The race started at the Freedom Leisure Centre, Chepstow, at 8pm in the evening, so it was already dark. David had already decided he was not going to run at the start. Two days before the event he had woken up with a sore throat and for the next 48 hrs leading up to the race he had not felt 100%. He didn't tell anyone apart from Ann. There was never any question of him backing out as he would have let too many people down. However, with a potential infection developing, he was certainly not going to push himself from the start. Conservation of energy was the key, which was fine with me as I would get an easier ride.

When the gun went off 84 competitors ran off into the night while we followed walking.

The first night went well. David was determined not to have to get his maps out and to follow others. There were plenty of people to follow. He got us into a group of 20 competitors so no navigational problems ensued. No one appeared to be using poles, keeping them stowed away for later. A strange decision as surely the easier you make the miles at the start the better you will feel towards the end. David and I knew that but we seemed to be the only ones.

David and I were just able to keep up with the back markers who were running the down hills and flats but walking the up hills. However, David was on his walking limit and was working me hard.

There were no views to be seen along the Wye Valley as it was pitch black, but we did have a clear sky with thousands of stars twinkling down on us and the sounds of owls hooting to keep us company.

The first check point at Monmouth (19 miles) was reached just after 12:30am, over 2 hours up on schedule. David left me outside, then made his usual quick stop, getting his water topped up and eating whatever looked appealing.

We were soon back on our way and heading through the town centre. There were a few locals who'd had a little too much and were trying to find their way home or to another bar. We kept our distance and David did not stab me into the ground quite so hard so we did not draw attention to ourselves. It's a good job he wasn't wearing his Scooby Doo suit.
Unfortunately we had left the checkpoint on our own so David had to get his Satmap handheld satellite navigation unit out and start navigating for himself. As he only has two hands he can't use me when navigating so I get carried.

He kept on course through the woods and farm land, before reaching White Castle which could be barely made out, from his head torch beam. A few other competitors were going past him but the majority were now walking most of the time so we were starting to overtake. Shortly after leaving White Castle we were treated to a spell binding sight as the moon rose casting its mysterious light across the landscape. It looked enormous, being close to the horizons and it certainly made us stop and stare at this magical sight. I was half expecting Harry Potter to fly past on his Nimbus 2000 broom stick (I often dreamt of being a flying pole).

Before long we were descending into the town of Pandy and walking along the main road to Checkpoint 2 at the village hall. It was 6am and still dark. We had covered 36 miles at this point. Some competitors were choosing to sleep at this checkpoint but David wanted to fuel up and get going. We stayed for about 15 mins. He left me outside and I managed to get a few words with another set of poles. It appeared that more competitors were getting their poles out now, which was more company for me.

We left Pandy at 6.30am and started on the long climb up to the Black Mountains. As we climbed off to the east the sun was just rising and we were treated to a breath-taking sunrise. David loved a good sunrise as it was a sign that darkness had been banished and the day was starting. He'd seen enough in his time, often getting up at 'silly o' clock' to undertake some physical activity. Just a shame I never got to share them. But I was sharing this one and it felt good. We were on the top of the world (well the Black Mountains at least) and covering the ground well, with no worries or troubles.

At the trig point David stopped to get a picture of the Pole Angels. He leant me up against the side of the trig point but in the wind I couldn't get a proper grip so down I went crashing to the ground. David wasn't giving up and moved around to the sheltered side of the trig point to try again. Why didn't he do that the first time, I thought? That would have saved me a few scratches. I was certainly starting to show my age. But I stood up straight and tall for the photo so the Angels looked at their best.

The high point of the King Offa's Dyke run at 531m, standing to attention despite a stiff breeze.

David emailed the picture back to Ann so it could be out on the sands Facebook site so the Pole Angel families could see the progress made so far. As he did this he noticed another 4 names had come through to be added to the poles: Ruby Jayne, Aaron, Sasha and Flyn (They were later added to the poles at Knighton).

From the trig point we followed the Hatterall Ridge along the Black mountains, which basically is the border between England and Wales, but neither were visible as fog had come down to spoil our views. There were no other competitors in sight so David had to keep checking his Satmap device. He had walked Offa's Dyke 17 years previously, taking just over a week. He couldn't remember too much about the route but he did remember continuing on the Black Mountains past Hay Bluff and missing the path down to Hay-on-Wye. Back in those days, way before I was manufactured, there were no satellite navigation devices, only a map and compass and David would often argue with his compass, not realising that the compass was always right and he was wrong.

This time he took his time, found the correct path off the ridge and no time was lost. We were soon heading into Hay-on-Wye, the second hand bookshop capital of the world. David knew the way to the checkpoint at the Parish Hall but the organisers had signposted it. The time was 11:30am.

Hay-on-Wye was the first major check point, at 50miles. We spent 30 mins here. I was left outside as usual while David got hot food, changed his socks and applied blister plasters. He then restocked his food and drink supplies in his rucksack before heading out.

While I was outside I learnt from other poles that there had been quite a few dropouts already. This surprised me as we were barely a quarter of the way through the event and the weather had been kind to us, with no rain. I put this down to under use of poles. Yes poles were the answer to everything and that was why David and I were getting on fine.

The next section proved to be a little bit more testing for David. In fact it was really tough. He met up with Simon shortly after the checkpoint. Simon had no poles for me to chat to but he was a very quick walker and David tried to keep up with his pace but couldn't. Simon slowly disappeared into the distance.

Two days before the start David had got a sore throat and did not feel brilliant when he started the race. A mixture of excitement and adrenaline had made him forget his medical problems but I did notice the odd cough which was getting more frequent as the event went on. I only know this because I hate being coughed over. All that saliva landing on you, it's not nice.

It was early afternoon by now and the weather was quite muggy. I could tell from my cork handles that David had started to sweat profusely. He started resting his head on any metal object he came across, such as a gate, to try and cool himself down. Then he started to convince himself that he was coming down with a serious infection and would have to drop out. All his demons came out to taunt him. No sleep for over 24 hours was not helping the situation. He felt awful and he could see no way of finishing. David was certain that he would have to retire and make his excuses. The race organisers would probably pull him out anyway and chastise him for starting such an event with a chest infection. He'd done over 60 miles in 18 hours which wasn't bad but it was time to call it a day.

David's pace had slowed and he was expecting others to come past him. He kept looking round for them, a sure sign of weakness. I had to do something. I had to get him to focus on the reason he was doing this challenge, for the charities and those Pole Angels.

I craftily twisted in his hand and thrust my left tip into the air so it scraped along the side of his calf. He looked down in disgust but as he looked down his eyes caught sight of the Angels names I was proudly carrying. He digested this information (it took a while) then he began to think about the Angels and how, if he stopped he would be letting them down. The poor families had been through enough trauma and heartbreak and here he was, not keeping his end of the bargain. He had to get those Angels to the end, there was no other answer.

My plan had worked. No other runners did come past us so I guess they were also having a bad time. David started to work out an action plan which centred round a bizarre idea. He felt so bad that he knew he couldn't feel any worse, so he decided to start running. Yes after 60 miles of walking he picked me up, tucked me under his arm and we ran.

As he ran he started to feel a little better and a little stronger and I was ecstatic. We passed Simon who was surprised we were running. David was slowly getting back to his usual positive self.

We slowed to a walk for the climb up Hergest Ridge but I could tell with the way David was stabbing me into the ground he was feeling more his usual self. Then we ran the long descent into Kington and Checkpoint 4.

We had now covered 67 miles and it was 5:14pm. I was left outside the checkpoint and as David fed his face inside I saw Simon arrive. He must have run some of the way to have kept up with us. Surprisingly Simon was out of the checkpoint before David. I wondered whether David had accidentally fallen asleep. The plan was not to sleep till the next checkpoint at Knighton, which was over 14 miles away.

David finally exited the checkpoint and by the way he grabbed me I could tell he was determined to get to the next checkpoint before midnight and finally get some sleep there. Rain was also forecast for overnight so there was no time to lose. David soon caught Simon up. I think this was his plan due to his awful navigating skills.

Simon turned out to be an excellent navigator as well as a fast walker. David and I stuck with him as dusk turned into night. David and Simon chatted away but I had no one to talk to. I was content however, as David was in a positive mood and in Simon he had found a competent navigator who would not get him lost.

Approximately 8 miles from the next checkpoint, as it started to rain, we came across a lady competitor, Cristina. We had just struggled to find our way across a field in the dark. Cristina had become totally disorientated in the dark. She seemed mighty relieved to see us and joined our little group. Together the three of us marched on our way. Simon was at the front navigating, Cristina in the middle and David and I brought up the rear, looking out for threats, dangers and bogey men.

The rain persisted and the last few miles to Knighton seemed to needlessly go on for ever. Eventually we got to the Market Hall at Knighton, Checkpoint 5. It was just gone 10:30pm and we had covered 82 miles in just over 26 hrs. It was time to sleep.

For once David took me with him into the checkpoint. The Market Hall was strewn with other competitors lying like zombies in their sleeping bags. Every vantage point was taken, from comfy sofas to the hard wooden floor. You notice I used the description of sleeping bags as I could not see anyone with a liner. They had carried the extra weight and were now reaping the rewards. I was looking forward to seeing David snuggle down into his liner.

After feeding his face again David changed out of his wet clothes and hung them on a chair to dry. Unfortunately he missed the radiator in the corner. It was now time for some shut eye. One of the checkpoint marshals suggested he use a back room, which was much quieter than the main reception area they had entered but would mean sleeping on the wooden floor. David took his advice and opted for the back room.

The room was virtually pitch black. Out came the liner and David positioned the few dry clothes he had left under his back side and head then crawled into the sleeping bag liner. From my vantage point at the side of David I could see he was far from comfortable fidgeting around until he found the least painful position, but it wasn't long before he was snoring his head off. I'm not sure how he slept feeling so uncomfortable but feelings of fatigue must have been greater than the feelings of pain and cold he had.

An hour later and he was trying a half sitting position with his head and back against the wall. This is his classic 'consultation room sleeping position' as adopted each lunchtime at the pharmacy. This position worked for another hour before he reverted back to a more conventional horizontal position.

I was in stitches all this time. All the other competitors had their nice cosy sleeping bags cushioning them while David went through the book of 100 positions to fall asleep in.

Outside, as David slept, I could hear the rain hammering down on the market hall roof. I was glad we had not been out in that. A good soaking could well have sent David into another depressive episode and that was the last thing we needed. I'm sure if you asked him he would tell you he had planned his sleep stop to avoid the bad weather, having studied BBC weather on his iPhone the day before. I think it was more luck than judgement.

I reckon he got 3 hrs sleep before he decided to get up. It was 3.20am and by this time the main reception area was even more crowded with sleeping zombies or bedraggled zombies who wished they were asleep. As David stumbled around putting his still damp clothes on, he noticed the radiator in the corner which was now trying to dry out a multitude of clothing items from competitors who had come in from the heavy rain.

As David was preparing to leave so was Simon so they teamed up together. There was also another runner leaving at the same time, so when David grabbed me we had a team of three runners leaving at 4pm, exactly on time according to David's schedule. The rain was still falling but not as heavy as it had been.

David was surprised but rather pleased that Simon was still with him. He had expected Simon to have already left the checkpoint. David had never liked running at night over unfamiliar terrain in the middle of nowhere, so he was delighted to join forces with Simon.

This next section, Miles 80 to 100, were probably the toughest of the whole 185 mile route as regards constant climbing and descending. The first climb was up to Panpunton Hill and the lights of Knighton shimmered in the distance below them. It was soon clear that the other runner was quicker than Simon and David so he went on, leaving David and Simon on their own.

As the pair of them skirted Cwm-sanaham Hill, Simon made a rare navigational error and they missed the path down to the road crossing near Selley Hall. They were not the only ones. Simon realised his mistake and they descended through a thick blanket of ferns which had already been trampled down by runners ahead of them. The descent was steep and I stopped David from falling on several occasions. Simon did remarkably well to stay upright, having no poles.

Constant climbing and descending from one valley to another was taking its toll on David. He was struggling to keep up with Simon. He still felt tired due to his restless sleep overnight and he was not always walking in a straight line although I was trying my best to keep him on track. Also to keep up with Simon he had to do a little run every few minutes picking me up. If he had lost contact with Simon I think he would have struggled to keep going.

I did notice that when David did start running he moved quite well. I guessed this was because as he ran, he put pressure on different parts of his feet compared with when he was walking. This meant that running was actually less painful than walking for him and as I got a free ride it was certainly less painful for me. This was good news all round, but I could tell that David was holding back on the running. He wanted to get a few more miles done.

The first few hours before it got light were hard going. The only high point was passing the half way point on the route where David stopped to get a photo. He propped me up against the signpost which pointed in one direction to Chepstow and in the other to Prestatyn. Each destination was 88 miles away. We had got to half way after 34 hours. All we had to do now was repeat what we had already done. Simple. Knowing you had less distance to cover than you had already done was a huge psychological boost for David.

After my photo shoot he emailed the picture over to Ann so it could be put on the SANDS website. Then on we continued into the Clun Hills.

I could tell David was mighty relieved when dawn eventually broke and with it, his energy levels rose, and I was subjected to more vigorous stabbing. The rain may have stopped but the relentless Clun Hills continued with steep ascents and descents and David used me to good effect to haul himself up the slopes and then cushion his knees and legs in the down hills. We also got some decent sections where Offa's Dyke was clearly visible.

On one section we came across a rotting sheep carcass. The stench was not pleasant and David had hurried on by so not to inhale the rancid smell. Not the most appealing sight but I remember thinking if only I had been in the hands of Bear Grylls. He would have had that carcass stripped in minutes. He would have eaten what was left of the raw flesh and then used the coat as a sleeping bag. I decided it was probably a good idea that I was not in the hands of Bear Grylls.

Finally the hills relented and the terrain levelled out. In the distance we could see Montgomery and again that lifted spirits, knowing we were in touching distance of the 100 mile check point.

David had previously recced this part of the route so he knew the way into the town and the checkpoint. It was about the only bit of navigating he had done that morning, with Simon keeping us on course for the majority of the 20 miles.

As we approached the check point a fellow competitor came running past us. I could not believe the spring in his step and neither could David. He seemed so fresh as he effortlessly passed us; absolutely amazing after 100 miles of running. We arrived at Montgomery Activity Centre at 10.30am (100miles in 38.5 hrs).

Montgomery was the second major checkpoint and David had access to his 2nd drop bag. I was unceremoniously dumped outside again but I did have a few more poles to talk to. The 100 mile check point was also the finish of a second race which was taking part at the same time as ours. It was called the Mercian challenge and the other poles told me that the majority of athletes dropping out were from the 100 mile event. In fact only 6 would go on to finish (Cristina was the first lady).

David was able to change not only his socks but also his trainers as well. He had a larger pair to allow for his feet swelling. He also had elastic laces. I don't think he had learnt to tie shoe laces yet. If you ever see him he will either have slip on shoes or elastic laces, so I think that proves my point.

He checked his feet out and everything seemed OK as regards blisters, but to be honest he is so inflexible he wouldn't have been able to see what was really going on under his feet (you should see him do yoga, it's hilarious). He could see the start of one blister forming on the end of a toe, so soon had it covered by a blister plaster. He then applied a few more plasters to the plasters already on his feet. I swear he was about 1cm taller due to all these plasters. But his policy of 'You can't have too many plasters' appeared to be working and even the medics agreed with him. In fact the medics were getting a little frustrated after seeing many competitors who had not had much success in preventing blisters. The problem was once that blister had formed it would always be painful. (The medics over the course of the event used 80m of Kinesiology tape, 500 tablets of paracetamol / ibuprofen, 750ml of Vaseline, 100 Compeed plasters and 400ml of anti-chafing cream).

Simon took full advantage of the medic's skills to get his feet treated. David on the other hand got an instant ice pack from his drop bag, activated it and applied it to his knees for a few minutes purely as a precautionary measure. He didn't need to do this due to the hard work I had put in protecting them for 100 miles but if it gave him a morale boost then that was fine. David then changed his head torch batteries, filled his bum bag with food and tucked into a baked potato filled with beans and cheese which the check point volunteers had prepared for him.

I had given up on David and Simon when they eventually came out of the checkpoint. We had only planned to be at the check point for 30 minutes but 45 minutes had now passed since David had dumped me outside. However when I saw David had changed into T-shirt and shorts I knew he meant business for the next section ahead. His intentions were to run the flatter parts of the route which were coming up. He had mentioned this to Simon as they were coming into Montgomery and it looked as though he was ready to carry out his plan.

After David had lead us away from the checkpoint, Simon took over the navigating. This next section was the longest on the entire route with 20 miles to cover before Llanymynech Village Hall and Checkpoint 7. However at least half of this distance was following canals and the River Severn, so was dead flat. It was David's intention to run it.

The first significant land mark we came across was Beacon Ring, an Iron Age hill fort. At the fort was a sign explaining all about the fort, but what really caught David's attention was a map of the Offa's Dyke path with a 'You are Here' marker. The marker showed we were significantly nearer Prestatyn than Chepstow. It may have been just a sign but it was another huge morale booster to David. He picked me up and carefully laid me by the side of the sign so you could see all the Pole Angels. Then he took my picture and emailed it off to Ann so the Angel parents could see our progress.

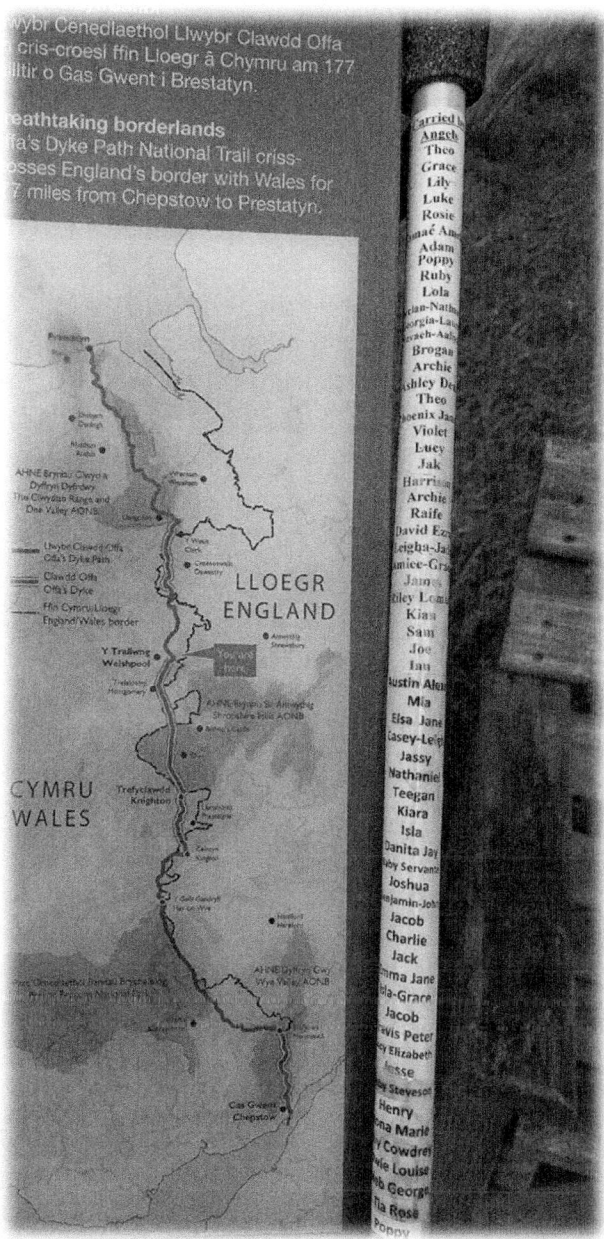

A great morale booster for David and the Angels as we were well over half way.

We descended from Beacon Ring and I felt our pace had dropped. I had also sensed that David was eager to start running and this perception was strengthened when we started to be passed by other competitors.

After the road crossing at Buttingham, David let Simon know he was going to start running as soon as they reached the Montgomery Canal. I think he was hoping Simon would say that he would run too, but Simon stayed quiet. The busy A483 was crossed and the canal reached. David said his goodbyes to Simon, picked me up and we were off running. David had a lot to thank Simon for, not least the navigating he had done over the last 20 hrs they were together.

The section along the Montogomery canal lasted barely a mile before the route left it and went across farm land to follow the River Severn. David was hoping that the route finding would be easy and luckily for him there were plenty of signs around, as well as a steady line of runners which we were now overtaking.

David kept on running and I kept on enjoying the ride. It was impressive to watch. After over 110 miles in his legs he was knocking out 9 minute miles. The only times we stopped were to climb over styles.

David's schedule had him reaching his overnight checkpoint at 2am. This meant he would only get 2 hrs sleep maximum if setting off again at 4pm. If he could maintain this running and spend as little time at the next checkpoint he could get to the overnight checkpoint earlier and get more rest, so on we ran.

We left the River Severn and headed over farm land, passing through Four Crosses before reaching the Montgomeryshire Canal. This was the final stretch before the checkpoint up ahead and David was determined to keep running. On we plodded desperately searching for the checkpoint signs to appear directing us off the canal, but there were none to be seen. It seemed to take for ever but eventually the first sign was reached and we diverted away from the canal and into the town.

Checkpoint 7 (120 miles) was at Llanymynech Village Hall which David and I had visited the previous month, when we checked out where Checkpoints 3 to 7 were (preparation is the key to success). It was a shame that David had totally forgotten where the checkpoint was. At the crossroads in the centre of the village the sign said to go straight on. And did we? No, David knew better and we turned right. After 5 minutes when the village hall did not appear where it should have been David admitted he was wrong and we turned round to follow the organisers' signs. 10 minutes wasted: When will he learn to trust others?

At the checkpoint I could tell David was in no mood to loiter. I was as usual deposited outside and after removing his shoes he went inside. 2 minutes later he was back out with half a cheese roll stuffed in his mouth and another one in his hand. Now that's what I call a quick pit stop.

It was 5:40pm so would be getting dark in less than an hour. David's intention was to keep moving quickly, running and walking now, until he came across the next competitor up ahead and then hopefully tag along with them. He knew the way out of the checkpoint, thankfully this part of his memory was working correctly, and with me safely tucked under his arms we quickly climbed out of the village and up wooded hillside of Fron-goch to the disused quarry.

Just as we were reaching the top David's luck was in because we caught two runners up, Richard and Peter. David greeted them with a "Hi".

Richard in true 'Blind Date' tradition said, "What's your name and where do you come from?"

David replied "I'm David and I'm from Chesterfield."

David knew he had met up with a great group of guys to run with and I was pretty pleased too, as both Peter and Richard both had poles for me to chat to.

I quickly learnt from Peter and Richard's poles that they had left Checkpoint 5, Knighton Community Centre, last night just before Simon and David arrived. They had then got caught in the heavy overnight rain. So while David was sleeping at the checkpoint they had found some shelter in a farmer's barn to change into their wet weather gear, then they had continued on through the deluge. I wasn't sure whether David had been very lucky, or very smart.

Our group of three runners and three sets of poles made good progress as the light was failing, running and walking through the Welsh countryside. But as day turned into night and darkness enveloped the landscape I could sense David struggling to keep up with the other two.

David would silently curse when Richard or Peter started to run as he didn't want to lose them. When an uphill gradient came and the other two slowed to a walk, David would be the only one in the group that was breathing heavily. Was this his chest infection beginning to make itself known or was he paying the price for running constantly the last 10 miles into Llanymynech. He really was having to work to keep up with the others and I was being stabbed harshly in the ground as we struggled at the back of the group. We both knew if we lost contact with Peter and Richard then we would have to self-navigate and would struggle to reach the next checkpoint before midnight.

As the group crested the top of one particular hill, Peter's phone rang. He answered it to find his wife on the other end desperate to talk to him. The wind was quite strong at this point so Peter very calmly told his wife he would call her back when they had got into a more sheltered location.

Peter was true to his word and he rang his wife back a few moments later. You could tell as the conversation unfolded that a family crisis was developing and Peter's wife needed his help there and then. Peter remained amazingly calm given the circumstances and was doing the best he could to help the situation, but there was only so much one can do on the side of a hill in the pitch black somewhere in the Welsh countryside.

The terrain we were covering involved climbing over many stiles, which was not great for tired legs. Poles and stiles do not get on very well and often we will fly erratically into the sky as our owner mounts the stile, endangering any other humans in the vicinity. The only way for a human to prevent getting jabbed is to keep their distance from the poles in front. The problem with this is the last person has to then quicken their pace to catch up. So after every stile David would have to break into a run to keep up with Peter and Richard.

Richard took the opportunity to call his wife as our pace had slowed a little. David was struggling still to keep up and breathing heavily, even though the other two were now chatting merrily away on their phones. I don't think he would have had the breath to have called Ann and if he had she may have wondered what all the heavy breathing was about and got the wrong idea totally.

As the night progressed David was digging deep into his energy reserves to keep up. Richard appeared to be strolling along, doing an excellent job route-finding and enjoying himself. Peter was doing his best to deal with his family crisis which seemed to be worsening as time went by. David knew this should be his last night running. He held this thought in his head. He told himself that if he lost contact with Peter and Richard he would die. A little alarmist I think you would agree, but it seemed to work. Stile after stile he followed the others, panting at the back of the group and using me to get every ounce of energy available to propel himself forward.

It was 15 miles from Llanymynech to Chirk Castle, Checkpoint 8, but it seemed like 50. It also seemed like there were a 1000 stiles to negotiate, although everyone's eyes were still intact.

As we neared Checkpoint 8, Peter's poles told me he was now struggling due to a combination of fatigue and concern over his family crisis. I could tell David was perking up a little as he started to believe he would make it to the checkpoint before midnight. Richard was his cheerful self, appearing to be effortlessly skipping along.

With a mile to go David and I recognised the terrain as we had been dropped off here in August, at the start of the recce. David let the others know we were almost at the checkpoint, with just a short climb up to the castle. The route was off the official Offa's Dyke path as the organisers had obtained special permission to go into the castle grounds. The three of them, complete with poles, climbed up to the castle, which unfortunately could not be seen in the darkness. The climb finally relented and the lights of the checkpoint could be seen. David was so relieved. It was 11.48pm, 135miles completed in 52hours. He hoped he would be at the finish line in Prestatyn by this time tomorrow.

As we came into the checkpoint there were two other runners just leaving. One of them was Chris Ette, who I had also seen leave Checkpoint 2 at Pandy as David and me arrived. Chris had presented David with his finisher's medal and T-shirt at the Quin last year. He was quite an accomplished ultra-distance athlete who David looked up to. David and Chris wished each other well before I was dumped outside and David went inside.

Through a tiny crack in the door I could just make out what was happening inside the checkpoint. There were three other competitors already at the checkpoint tucked up in their sleeping bags. The actual checkpoint, which was an out building adjacent to the actual castle, had at one point been a squash court. It still had the laminated wooden floor and white walls, complete with the line markings of the court.

David deposited his kit in an unoccupied space then checked out the food table to see what goodies it had to offer. After feeding his face and filling his water supply up ready for the morning, he made a start of sorting his kit out.

Richard came over to see what time David was planning to leave and they agreed a 4am departure (David really does like his 4's). David then changed out of his shorts as he reckoned he would be cold overnight in his sleeping bag liner. This simple operation was made to look almost impossible as David precariously tried to keep his balance putting his running tights on. Most people would have just sat down but that was too simple for him. The lady marshal at the checkpoint obviously felt sorry for David and his pathetic dressing strategy so she came over and helped him keep his balance while he put the tights on. In fact the lady could not have been more helpful, even asking David if he would like a wakeup call in the morning. Now that is service for you.

It was now time to start the sleeping bag liner position game. Out came all David's spare clothing to be used as a pillow and bottom cushion, then he wriggled into his liner and fidgeted around trying to find the most comfortable position. Eventually he got off to sleep. To my amazement the observant lady marshal noticed David was shivering and switched on a little electric fan heater. He was getting way too much attention while I stood patiently outside.

Me and all the poles were soon deep in conversation, well we had to do something while our owners slept. Some of these poles had done some amazing events, including the Ultra Trail du Mont-Blanc (110mile mountain marathon around Mont-Blanc with 10,000m of ascent), the pinnacle of many ultra-runners careers. I was jealous, but then none of the other poles had been given the honour of carrying Angels. No, I was no longer jealous. I was proud to be an Angel carrier and I showed off the names of the Angels to all the other poles.

The only time us poles were disturbed during the night was when David came out to answer the call of nature. It was pitch black outside and I could tell he had no intentions of going the 100 metres to the toilet block. It must have been a number 1 as he wasn't gone long. It was a good job no other runners were coming into the checkpoint at that time as his nocturnal activities may have been exposed.

David woke naturally just after 3.30am, so did not need his prearranged wake up call. As he got all his kit together and munched down a breakfast of crisps, sausage rolls and chocolate biscuits (good wholesome food) he was joined by Richard. The two of them left the checkpoint and were guided by another marshal up the path and on to the runner's route. Sadly Peter was not joining them. As a husband and father he knew these duties were more important than finishing the run so he sacrificed his race to be with his family at their time of need. I have no doubt he would have finished the race and I believe he has entered next year's already.

Richard and David set out in good spirits that morning. It may have been dark with dawn at least a couple of hours away, but they knew they would be finishing that day. David had done the route between the next two checkpoints before but, as I already knew, his memory had a few imperfections. Luckily Richard was an expert navigator, just using the map to keep on route.

I chatted away merrily with Richards's poles. Quite amusingly they told me that while David had spent the night on the wooden floor of the squash court, Richard had found the stairs to the viewing gallery. Being higher up it was significantly warmer and he even found some old sheets to act as cushioning to lie on. He'd had a most enjoyable nights rest. I hoped David did not find out about this as he may not have been too pleased.

It wasn't long before we were on the Llangollen Canal and we followed the unofficial route over the aqueduct (this was allowed by the organisers). In the daylight, a month previously, when we crossed over, it had been an impressive sight spanning the gorge over the River Dee with only a handrail on one side. Now in darkness it looked nothing special.

We kept up a good pace and as dawn broke we were skirting the impressive cliffs of the Ruabon and Eglwyseg Mountains. David's memory was not failing him as he helped to navigate. They dropped down onto the road at World End before climbing on to the lower slopes of Cyrn-y-Brain. The heather gave way to the Llandegla forest, which Richard flew down. I think he could smell the food at the next checkpoint.

By the time we got to Llandegla campsite and Checkpoint 9 it had just gone 8.45am and light rain was falling. Checkpoint 9 was very different to all the other checkpoints for two reasons.

1. It was an outdoor checkpoint which basically consisted of 3 large dome tents; 1 for the marshals, 1 for competitors and 1 for drop bags.

2. After receiving a huge welcome at all the other checkpoints there was a certain lack of friendliness and helpfulness. Probably not surprising as most people would be fed up, sat in a tent for 2 days in the rain.

As I mentioned earlier Richard could smell the good food coming from the marshal's tent when we arrived. As it was raining all the tents were zipped shut. Richard being a little more confident than David shouted a few hello's at the tent and when there was no answer he naturally unzipped the entrance and proceeded to walk in.

He was met with a stern voice saying "You can't come in here, this tent is just for us marshals. Your tent is over there."

Silly old Richard, fancy not knowing which tent was which, he had forgotten to read the invisible signs. One of the marshals came out and as he did so I could see all the food laid out on a table top inside their tent. David also saw it too.

We were led over to the drop bag tent, where David collected his third and final drop bag, and then shown to another tent which already had two runners inside. As Richard and David sat down in the tent the marshal asked them if they would like some hot food, which they both obviously did, then he disappeared.

As David and Richard and I (I actually got taken inside the tent) made ourselves comfortable we listened to the other two runners talk. I recognised one of them. He was the guy who had run past Simon and David as they approached the Montgomery checkpoint and David had commented on the unreal spring in his step. Well unfortunately the spring had gone and according to the Medics he had infected blisters and his race was over. The other runner was saying how pleased he was with his performance. He reckoned he would have made a top ten finish but he was pulling out as well now.

I could tell David found this last comment rather amusing. It's one thing to say you would have done something but it's a totally different thing to actually do it. Surely this runner should be disappointed as he had achieved joint last place by not finishing. I guess you can put a positive spin on anything.

David checked out his feet while waiting for his food and applied yet more blister plasters. He changed his wet socks for a dry pair, but I was sure the new pair would be ringing wet within the hour with the rain. Finally he activated another ice pack and put it over his knees. Let's call it a comfort blanket.

When the hot food arrived it was excellent and David wolfed it down in seconds. In fact I can't tell you what it was because it was devoured before I got to see. Richard's nose was obviously well trained.

David and Richard prepared to leave, getting their kit ready. David wanted to stock up on further food supplies and he had seen the table in the marshal's tent. He also wanted some orange to add taste to his water. Both requests seemed reasonable. As he got to the marshal's tent they opened it a small amount so he could get his arm in but he felt rather intimidated and just took a biscuit. When he asked for orange squash to dilute his water he was told that they were virtually out and there were at least another 60 competitors to come through the checkpoint. Now David knew there had been many retirements, there were two sitting in the tent next to where they were standing. He also knew that Richard and he were probably in the top twenty. It therefore seemed highly unlikely that 60 more runners would be arriving at the checkpoint (28 runners actually followed us into Checkpoint 9). There was also the simple answer that you could go and buy some more. David politely bit his lip, said nothing and thanked the marshal.

Richard and David left the campsite and as they walked away it was clear neither were impressed with their hospitality. In fact Richard was still hungry and when they saw a shop open in Llandegla Richard darted in to buy supplies. He even bought David a sausage roll and can of coke, then put his change into the charity box. What a great guy.

Richard and David joked about the campsite checkpoint for the next few miles. It helped take their minds off the persistent drizzle of rain. They also discussed finishing and Richard stated he had wanted to finish in 72 hours originally but obviously that wasn't going to happen now. David however disagreed. He thought 72 hours was possible. They then set out with a new purpose, to finish within 72 hours. We poles certainly knew about it as we were pushed hard.

The next section we came to was a series of Iron Age hill forts known as Moels. It was another section of constant ascents and descents but at least they were not as severe as the Clun Hills had been. David had already walked this section in August but it was Richard's first time in the area. He was absolutely loving it and said he would definitely return at a later date.

Moel y Plas came first, followed by Moel Llanfair, Moel Gyw and Moel Eithinen. The views were not as good as they had been when David and I had done this section. It had been clear blue skies and in the distance you could see the sea ahead of you. Now it was just a misty horizon but Richard was still loving it and in doing so he was pushing the pace. David and I were pushing hard to keep up.

On the next section to Foel Fenili we lost our way. Richard had the ingenious idea to use the tracker devices all competitors had been given to locate where we were. He rang his wife Hayley and asked her to check our current position. Hayley dutifully obliged and between the two of them they worked out where we all were. David tried to use his Satmap but as he had not used it for many hours it was taking an age to load up. In other words David gave no help whatsoever.

Richard decided to get us back on track we needed to cross a field which was surrounded by a barbed wire fence. Climbing a barbed wire fence is difficult enough for David when he is fresh. But with heavy legs that had covered 160 miles it was significantly more difficult. I was thrown over with no regard for my safety, then David climbed up the fence and jumped over. Luckily no damage was sustained to either David or the fence.

We got back on the route and continued with Richard pushing the pace. As we neared Moel Famau with its Jubilee Tower in the summit David spotted two walkers ahead. Both he and Richard discussed whether they were competitors in the race or recreational walkers out for a stroll. It was difficult to tell, but we would know the answer pretty soon as we were rapidly gaining ground on them.

Just before we reached the Jubilee Tower we caught them. It was Chris and another competitor, Mick, who had been leaving Chirk Castle the previous night just as David, Peter and Richard were arriving. I grabbed a quick word with Chris's poles. He said they were making steady progress and expected to finish before midnight.

At the Jubilee Tower we stopped for some photos, Richard getting a selfie with all four runners in. There was a sign saying Prestatyn 20 miles, it was a huge morale boost for David. Then I noticed a mischievous look on Richards face. He asked David to push the pace so we could get out of sight of Chris and his companion as quickly as possible. David agreed and we upped the pace again, running virtually the whole way past Moel Dywyll and Moel Llys-y-coed to the road crossing.

There was just one more Moel to go now before dropping down to the village of Bodfari, Moel Arthur. David and I put on a little spurt so as to get ahead of Richard. David wanted to take a photo at the top but he did not want to slow Richard down.

When we got to the top David thrust me into the top of the summit cairn on Moel Arthur. I did get a few more scratches but I wasn't too bothered. David was taking a photo of me with my Pole Angels. This was another moment to savour. I wonder if any other poles have had such a moment? I doubt it.

Pole on a Moel.

From Moel Arthur we traversed the remaining few miles to Bodfari, dropping down to cross the A541 main road. Then it was stab, stab, and stab, up the track on the other side as David drove my steel tips into the Tarmac. I was apprehensive about getting lost on the way to the checkpoint, which was barely a mile away. This was not helped when initially Richard said to ignore the first sign post the organisers had put out for the runners. Richard however soon got his bearing after David questioned his decision and shortly afterwards we made it to the Bodfari Woodland Skills Centre, Checkpoint 10. We had covered 169 miles and it was 4.17pm.

If Checkpoint 9 had been a little standoffish, Checkpoint 10 was too accommodating. Again I was left outside with Richards's poles. Richard and David were having their orders taken as they walked through the door. David ordered banana sandwiches and the different options were checked. Brown or white bread, butter or margarine, mashed or sliced banana, crusts on or off, squares or triangles, pre-chewed or non-chewed. David thought he was hallucinating and was now at the Ritz in London, such was the standard of service.

Next came the 2nd course of beef curry. David hadn't quite finished his sandwiches so he mixed them into the curry. It tasted good to him but then he does have weird tastes.

David then popped off to the toilet. I'm not sure what happened during the next 15 mins, yes 15 mins, although the smell emanating from under the door was horrific. I guess all the high energy foods he had consumed had to come out at some time but they certainly took their time. I think Richard thought David had actually fallen asleep on the toilet.

By now Richard's poles and I were getting quite impatient. This break had been scheduled for half an hour so we had enough time to get to the finish in the light. When the pair of them finally reappeared the whole checkpoint pit stop had taken nearly an hour. We had 3 hours to cover the 12 miles to Prestatyn and finish within Richards target time of 72 hrs. It was going to be close.

The checkpoint marshals very kindly walked us up to where the official path started. On the way out, one of them noticed that David's head torch was desperately clinging to the open pocket of his rucksack. He mentioned this to David who asked him to secure it, so he did. The volunteers wished us well and we were on our way with a deadline to keep.

David was desperate to get Richard to the end in his goal time as he knew without Richard's help he would probably be lost on a Moel many miles behind. David attacked the route ahead with such vigour it sent shock waves right through me. He had already removed his waterproof jacket to show how serious he was, not holding anything back. This was going to be a sprint finish.

While Richard had been the strongest of the pair since they had met almost 24 hours ago, now the roles were reversed. David set the pace and Richard followed shouting out the odd directional message to keep David on course. We were covering the ground well but the numerous stiles we were encountering were unfortunately slowing us down.

We skirted the Clwydian Range and crossed the footbridge over the busy A55 trunk road at Rhuallt. After a small road section we were back crossing fields and stiles with us poles trying not to get in the way of either David or Richard. At Marian Ffrith we got our first good view of the sea and David quickly got a picture as Richard carried on running.

Then disaster struck. We had entered a field with David and me leading, but we lost the path and couldn't see a route out. The far end of the field had prickly gorse around its border. Richard thought the exit was in the corner but when David and I went to check we could not see a way through. We back tracked and basically went round in circles for 10 minutes, with Richards's language getting more colourful by the minute.

Richard took the decision to jump the drystone wall and go around the field. Given the dilapidated state of the wall it looked as though we weren't the only people who had done this over the years. When we reached the corner of the field, Richard had been right, the exit was there but it was very overgrown. David felt as though he had let Richard down.

The light was starting to fail now. Prestatyn was tantalisingly close. We could see it in the distance but the route was teasing us, taking us along the last remains of the Clwydian Range. It then started to rain, making it slippery underfoot, which wasn't helping when trying to run in poor light. I was doing my best to make sure David stayed upright.

Richard quickly put his head torch on. David went for his but it was stuck. The volunteer at the last checkpoint had done a really good job at securing it. In fact he had done such a good job that in the gloomy light David could not see how he had tied it on. Richard came to the rescue giving David a small light to use. It was not as good as a head torch but it wasn't bad.

We continued, then the route doubled back on itself and Richard got doubts as to whether they had taken a wrong turn. He rang Hayley for help and she confirmed that we were still on course. While Richard was on the phone David eventually freed his head torch. But when he went to turn it on nothing happened. Unfortunately when he changed the batteries at one of the previous checkpoints he had put one of them in the wrong way. With Richard shining his light over him, David had to open the cover and check all the batteries until he found the offending one and changed its position. Light at last but the 72 hour time goal had been lost with all this faffing around.

The pair of them descended into Prestatyn and I could sense David's disappointment for letting Richard down. As soon as we hit proper Tarmac I was under David's arm, and Richard and David made a charge for the finish line. It was over a mile to the finish and they had to climb the steps of the footbridge over the railway line. As they came down the other side the finish was in sight. They both sprinted like fools, with the race organiser Richard Weremiuk (Richard W) there to greet them. We all reached the finishing stone at 8:14pm. It had taken us 72 hours and 14 minutes to run the 185 miles of King Offa's

Dyke. We were the 14th and 15th finishers. We may have missed Richard's target time, but David had beaten his own schedule by 4 hours and the cut off time by 24 hours.

Richard W took our picture. We had got the Pole Angels to the finish. I was relieved, shattered and immensely proud.

Richard W led David and Richard into the leisure centre next to the finish, which was acting as the race headquarters. They both dug deep into their rucksacks and fished out the small coin they had been given at registration before the race began. I was amazed David hadn't lost his, due to his poor track record for losing items.

David had joked with Richard during the race that the finishing memento they were going to receive was a car. It wasn't quite, but it was a lovely silver trophy in the shape of Wales with the KOD route marked on it. It was certainly the best trophy David had received in his running career. He took my picture with the Pole Angels next to the trophy, a most satisfying moment indeed.

We were shown into a room which the organisers were using to store all the kit bags and I was again unceremoniously dropped to the floor while David went to find his bags. But I didn't care, my job was done, it was time to rest.

In the morning when it was light, David took me back to the finish stone to get some more photos of the Pole Angels. Then we went to the beach, which was literally just a few metres further on. David and Richard had joked on the last day of KOD that they were going to finish by running into the sea. It never happened, I think both of them were too tired.

That morning David securely planted me in the Prestatyn Sand and took my picture. In the morning sunlight, as the waves lapped at my tips, I proudly displayed the Pole Angels I had been given the honour of carrying, as well as our sponsors from the pharmacy. I was the luckiest poles in the world.

Framing the finishing stone at the end of King Offa's Dyke run.

Chapter 11.

My final journey

If there ever comes a day when we can't be together, keep me in your heart, I'll stay there forever - Winnie the Pooh

After finishing the race David had managed to get washed and fed before crashing out on the floor of one of the gym rooms in the leisure centre. I was glad he was now smelling a little better. After getting all the photos he could think of with me and the Pole Angels in the morning, we just had to wait for his 3rd drop bag to get back from Checkpoint 9.

While we waited we cheered home other runners who were finishing. Chris who we had last seen at Jubilee Tower, finished in 75hrs 52 mins. He and Mick were the next two runners to finish after Richard and David. Simon finished in 82 hours. In all there were 44 finishers and 29 retired. The winners took just over 52 hours.

When David got his final drop bag it was just after 11am. He had a large holdall with all his drop bags in, a rucksack and me to carry to the station. Google maps said he would have to catch four trains to get back home to Chesterfield at that time of day. He didn't want to wait around any longer than necessary. His cough was getting worse and he'd booked a GP appointment later that day. He was also desperate to see his wife, Ann.

So the complicated train journey began. First up was Prestatyn to Chester. Luckily the train was quite empty at that time of day. He lugged the holdall onto the luggage rack at the end of the carriage he had entered, found the nearest seat and deposited me on the overhead rack. He then feel soundly asleep. Luckily he woke up a few minutes before the train arrived at Chester. He had slept through the stations in between.

He grabbed his rucksack and me and then lugged the holdall off the train. We had a 20 minute wait until picking up his next train to Crewe. Again he was lucky the train was not too full as he lugged all his bags and me onto it. It was only a 20 minute journey from Chester to Crewe and he didn't have much time to rest before the weight lifting routine with me and his bags restarted.

Crewe was a large station and it took him a while to work out which platform to catch his next train to Stockport from. On arriving at the platform he dumped me and all the bags just inside a café and bought some food for the next leg of his journey.

At 2:11pm we boarded the Virgin train bound for Stockport. It was the third train of the day. The holdall went in the luggage rack at the end of the carriage and I was again deposited on the overhead luggage rack. David then settled down to eat his recently purchased food.

The train came into Stockport station at 2:36pm and David prepared to leave again. He put his rucksack on, got the holdall from the luggage rack and stepped off the train. It was the last time me and the Pole Angels saw him.

The Pole Angels and I carried on to Manchester Piccadilly. I can't tell you where we went after that, the Pole Angels have sworn me to secrecy. They were desperate to continue their adventures. Obviously they would have liked to have been with David but they knew he spent too much time at work, so it was time to go it alone.

So the Pole Angels and I are out there having fun. I'm taking good care of them, like I did with David, and I'll make sure they won't come to any harm. Don't come looking for us because you'll never find us and you wouldn't want the Pole Angels adventure to end, would you?

Epilogue

David realised he had left his poles shortly after boarding his final train to Chesterfield. He arrived home later that day having lost no more items of kit. He also managed to survive his chest infection after two courses of antibiotics.

He made extensive enquiries to try and find the poles by phone and email. Ann and David also visited the lost property at Manchester Piccadilly a week later, which is where the poles should have ended up had the train cleaning company found them.

As a last resort, after a suggestion from one of his SANDS friends, he posted a picture of the poles and their Angels on Facebook. To this day the poles have still not been found. The Facebook post was shared as far away as New Zealand.

The King Offa's Dyke run that David ran with the Pole Angels raised £2104, split between the charities of Ashgate Hospice, Chesterfield Multiple Sclerosis Society and Chesterfield SANDS.

David continues to raise money for all these charities in various different ways. He is currently looking for a new set of poles to help him.

David and I hoped you enjoyed reading this book. If you would like to get in touch with David, for whatever reason, you can do so at anndavidsmith@icloud.com

He currently has a justgiving page where he lists future events and updates:
www.justgiving.com/grumpygrandad
You can follow his training or lack of it on Strava

The Individual Pole Angel Stories.

The next part of this book is given over to the Angels who appeared on the walking poles.

I tried to contact all of the parents to give them the opportunity to tell their Angel's story. I gave no guidelines, it was entirely up to them exactly what they wrote, whether it be a single character or a 1000 word story. I felt it right for them to have the recognition they deserve. They made the poles special and without them there would be no story.

Each Angel has a page regardless of whether a story was submitted or not. The omission of a story for an Angel could be down to many reasons one of which being simply that I was unable to contact them. Some are anonymous.

The accounts cover many aspects of baby loss. They are real, have undergone minimal editing and will probably make you cry.

The Angel stories are in the order which they appeared on the Angel Poles which was as follows:-

Theo, Grace, Lily, Luke, Rosie, Esmaé Amelia, Adam, Poppy, Ruby, Lola, Declan-Nathaniel, Georgia-Lauren, Nevaeh-Aaliyah, Brogan, Archie, Ashley Dean, Theo, Phoenix James, Violet, Lucy, Jak, Harrison, Archie, Raife, David Ezra, Leigha-Jade, Amiee-Grace, James, Riley Lomas, Kian, Sam, Joe, Ian, Austyn, Mia, Elsa Jane, Casey-Leigh, Jassy, Nathaniel, Teegan, Kiara, Isla, Danita Jay, Baby Servante, Joshua, Benjamin-John, Jacob, Charlie, Jack, Emma-Jane, Isla-Grace, Jacob, Travis Peter, Lucy Elizabeth, Jesse, Baby Steveson, Henry, Leona Marie, Baby Cowdrey, Zowie Louise, Caleb George, Tia Rose, Poppy, Ryan Aaron, William Roy, Ashley, Ruby Jayne, Aaron, Sasha, Flyn

First up is my grandson Theo.

Theo

Theo Benjamin Chaplen was born asleep on the 1st September 2014, I was 42 weeks pregnant. This affected my whole family. My mum and my stepdad have been my rock all the way. We remember Theo every day and we talk about him every day. He will never be forgotten.

My step dad David Smith does a lot of fundraising for SANDS and in memory of Theo. It's so important to get these poles back to David as they hold so much sentimental value to us all. We want to get our angels home.

Raising awareness and money for the SANDS charity is so important to us, as it's a brilliant charity for support and help to us angel parents and our families. I've found comfort in this charity and I've made some good friends through SANDS. It's a place we can talk about our experiences and remember our babies.

Nicola Chaplen

Nanny Struggles

In 2014 I was overjoyed to hear my oldest daughter, Tracey, was expecting her first child then out in of the blue my youngest daughter, Nicola, also told me she was expecting her first child. Told in confidence, I couldn't tell anyone until they made their own announcements.

After their scans the news came out both were expecting boys, one on the 14th August and the other on 19th August, exciting times lay ahead. Tracey's pregnancy went very smoothly with not many problems and an extremely good midwife who listened and acted on any worries she had. Nicola had a horrendous pregnancy being sick morning till night losing over one stone in weight. The midwife wasn't bothered and never really listened to her and even when I expressed my concerns she ignored me. Nicola would say, "They know what they are doing, it's ok."

Tracey gave birth to her 9lb 1oz son, Thomas, on 10th August but not without problems. It was a long labour and he had breathing difficulties. He had to go onto the special baby care unit for a week.

Once he was discharged home family life then began for them.

Nicola, in the meantime was still waddling round but having reduced movements, which wasn't being taken seriously by the midwife. She just said, "There isn't a lot of room in there for him to move."

I went with Nicola to her last midwife appointment asking if she could be taken in and induced as she was 42 weeks pregnant and I was due to go on holiday the following week. I so wanted to be with her but she said, "No". Being a little disheartened we left as we didn't think we could do anything about it.

That weekend our lives were going to change for ever. Nicola hadn't felt her baby move so I rang the triage unit explaining what the problem was and was told to take her straight up there. Once we had arrived she thought she felt him move but the midwife struggled to find a heartbeat. We were shown to another room and an ultrasound scan was performed and those words will haunt me forever, "I am so sorry, baby doesn't have a heartbeat. Your baby has gone."
We just looked at each other and I just asked if she ever makes mistakes but was told no. I frantically started to ring round,

first her partner then her dad. I needed someone else to be with us.

The labour was long and painful. Just watching my baby daughter in all that pain and knowing she wasn't going to get a happy ending was so heart-breaking, but also hoping they had got it all wrong.

I went into theatre with Nicola as she needed a forceps delivery. As soon as Theo was born Nicola passed him to me. Nicola had the biggest smile on her face, so proud of this little boy, Theo, her son. I cuddled him wishing him to breathe or cry. He was beautiful. Everyone in theatre had tears rolling down their faces.

We returned back to the ward where he was weighed. He was 7lb 7oz exactly the same as Nicola had been. He was just like her. I helped the nurse bathe him and then dress him, while my husband took lots of photos for Nicola. We asked if the hospital could arrange a blessing for him.

That evening all close family members arrived for the blessing. Nicola wanting to show off Theo but everyone was reluctant to look at him, let alone hold him. The look of sadness filled her face and broke my heart. I picked him up and cuddled him but no one else seemed bothered.

Both Nicola and her partner stayed with their son for 48 hours. We made sure they had food, money and our support at all times. We knew before she returned home we had to remove as much baby equipment as we could from her house and tell close friends and neighbours what had happened. Boy, I had no idea how hard it would be saying those words, "Nicola has lost the baby" but we had to do it.

We had to arrange Theo's funeral and that's when everything became difficult. Family thought they knew better and started to tell Nicola what she should do. They forgot it wasn't their son but Nicola's. We were yet again the bad guys.

We sat and listened to what Nicola wanted and took her down to the undertaker. We arranged for Theo to have the funeral his mummy wanted and had it conducted down to every last fine detail for her.

It then started. I was to get lots of grief from others saying I was turning Theo's funeral into a side show. It had become upsetting for them and the photos were disgusting. They asked, "What were you thinking of?"
My simple answer was, "Nicola!"

The next year became nearly impossible. If Tracey and Thomas were at my house Nicola wouldn't come, she couldn't bear to look at him. Every event became more painful; first birthday; first Christmas. When Tracey asked Nicola to be Thomas's godmother she said yes but how she held it together I'll never know.

We would often make late night trips up to the baby garden at the grave yard with Nicola so she could be with Theo.

When I think back I was unable to grieve for my grandson. I had to be the strong and support my daughter. Whether it was day or night she knew she could come and ask for help.

It felt at times I was a referee keeping the peace. It should never have been like that. You expect family to be more supportive but that wasn't to be.

Unfortunately I missed out on a lot of Thomas's first year but I had to make a difficult decision. No one else was helping

Nicola, they just said, "Life goes on" and I think they expected her to carry on as normal.

The day Theo was born my daughter's life changed forever. A tiny part of her was also lost forever.

Ann Smith

Grace

Grace Snowdon - Born Sleeping 8 October 2005.

My pregnancy with Grace was not an easy one. In fact getting pregnant proved to be a challenge in itself! We tried for months, being referred to fertility clinics and coming to terms with the fact that it might never happen (we even bought a dog!). On 1 March 2005 I stared in disbelief at the positive pregnancy test in my hand. Over the following months I suffered from lots of niggles and conditions that are a 'possibility' in pregnancy. Sickness, carpal tunnel, hip dysfunction, rhinitis, bleeding gums.....the list went on. It seemed I was getting all the symptoms in one go! I even wondered why people ever had more than one child! Oh how naive I was.

Fast forward to 6 October. I was 36 weeks and huge. I was uncomfortable and couldn't wait to give birth and finally meet my baby after all the weeks of discomfort, which had been exacerbated by the very hot summer. I remember that I felt as though I was coming down with flu; everything ached. I'd spent most of the day in bed sleeping as I'd not felt too good.

At 8pm it dawned on me that I had not felt my baby move much that day. I didn't immediately panic as I had seen the midwife the day before and everything had been fine. I smiled as I remembered hearing the heartbeat. By 8.30pm there had still been no movement and I began to worry. Towards the end of my pregnancy, my baby always had a big shuffle around, between 8pm and 8.30pm, every evening without fail.

At 8.45pm I rang the hospital in a panic. They told me not to worry but to come in so they could check me over. My husband was away on business so I called a friend and asked her to take me to the hospital. I still don't know why I didn't just drive myself there.

At the hospital the midwife tried to listen to my baby's heartbeat but was struggling to find it. I wasn't worried. I'd heard it only yesterday. She asked if there was usually a problem finding the heartbeat. I said there wasn't. She said the Doppler was an old model and probably playing up and they would take me for a scan instead.

I was moved to a side room where a doctor came to perform the scan. I can still remember him showing me the screen...."there's baby's head....." then going quiet and a look of concentration coming over his face. As he moved the wand around on my stomach, I remember thinking "There's no heartbeat, I can't see a heartbeat". I knew before he told me, "I'm sorry Mrs Snowdon but there is no heartbeat. Your baby has passed away." I was stunned.

I was told that I could go home and wait for labour to start naturally or I could be induced. I couldn't bear the thought of my baby dead inside me so I opted for the induction. My friend took me to my mum's, where I broke the news to her, and then my mum took me home to pick up my labour bag. This was all wrong. It shouldn't be like this.

The hospital rang my husband and told him he needed to get to the hospital, but wouldn't tell him what had happened over the phone. He had to take the slow train from London, knowing in his heart that something was terribly wrong. When he arrived at the hospital, I had to tell him the news.

I spent that night on the maternity unit in a separate room especially for parents in our situation. The next day I was taken to the labour ward and started treatment to induce labour. I spent two days on the ward until at 7.45pm on 8

October, my waters broke. My beautiful sleeping Angel was born just an hour later: Perfect in every way, except she never took a breath.

We asked for the hospital chaplain to perform a blessing service and arranged for close family to come in and meet our daughter. We called her Grace. Then came the hardest thing ever. I had to leave that room and leave my baby girl there. My heart was broken. It will never be the same.

Eleven years later, the pain is still there. It never goes away but you do learn how to live with it, how to channel the pain into energy to do something more positive, like running for charity. In 2015, the 10th anniversary of Grace's birth, I ran ten 10km runs plus a half marathon for SANDS. It was at one of these runs that I met the lovely people from Chesterfield SANDS, including Scooby Doo (aka David Smith). They took me under their wing and looked after me. My next challenge is to run the Yorkshire Marathon on 8 October 2017, Grace's 12th birthday.

Grace taught me just how strong I can be, what I can achieve if I put my mind to it, just what I can overcome and how it's pointless to sweat the small stuff. None of it really matters. I now have a gorgeous son, Rhys, born 18 months after his big sister. I have always made sure he knows of her existence, that he has a sister who is an "Angel-star" watching over us all.

Carmen Snowdon

Lily

WITHOUT LILY – In memory of Lily Walters 11/02/10

Lily Walters was born on Thursday the 11th February 2010 at 9.38pm. She was 23 weeks and 6 days gestation, or 6 months into my pregnancy and weighed 550g. She had Down's syndrome, severe AVSD (a huge hole in the heart that covered all 4 chambers), Esophageal Atresia (pipe taking food from mouth to stomach not connected/missing) and no stomach……she had a broken body incompatible with life. Lily was my one and only daughter. Because Lily was born a day under 6 months or 24 weeks, I have no papers, no registration or no certificate to say she was ever born. In the eyes of the law, Lily never existed.

I could write about the lack of care I had, the lack of support I received after, the hurt, the anger, the why's and what if's. I could speak about the dark days, the low times, the emptiness, but what good would that do? Except make me sad all over again.

I want to tell you about how such a tiny, tiny baby that touched my life so briefly has changed my life forever and that makes me smile with the very mention of her name. Losing Lily gave me a passion for helping others, she gave me the strength to speak out and the courage to do things I never dreamed I would do.

Without Lily I would be your normal mother, doing the school runs, oblivious to others around me. I would take my children for granted, I would probably dismiss their wanting to talk, wanting to cuddle and probably say 'I'm too busy' whenever they want my attention.

Without Lily, I would never understand how precious every baby and every child is. I would not appreciate the beauty around me, the things beyond the mundane day to day life. I would not understand how precious time is and how precious life is.

Without Lily, I wouldn't understand the amazing work not only our charity does, but every other charity in the country and beyond. I wouldn't appreciate the endless hours that normal everyday people give up to help their cause and help others, be it fighting cancers, helping defenseless animals, battling mental illness that can't be seen and so many more.

Without Lily I wouldn't have had the chance to step into Number 10 Downing Street, to attend the Mayor of Chesterfield's Christmas party. I wouldn't have swum in a freezing cold lake in the middle of the Lake District, waded through mud, climbed walls, nets and muddy hills!

Without Lily I wouldn't have run in the streets or around lakes, complete a half marathon or scale mountains. I wouldn't have attended prestigious events, met famous people or be spotted by local dignitaries who know who I am!

Most of all Without Lily I wouldn't have met all the amazing people that she has given me the opportunity to meet. Without Lily I wouldn't have lost the friends that I did, but gain the amazing and wonderful friends I have in my life now.

Without Lily I wouldn't have crossed these paths and never realized how people can come through such devastation to become so strong and so inspirational and so amazing.

Without Lily I wouldn't be the person that is here today. And yes……I would click my fingers and have her here with me in a heartbeat, and you all say that it will never happen…but in a way it has.

You see…. I am not Without Lily. She is in my heart, she is in my thoughts every waking hour, she is in my dreams at night, she is with me everywhere I go and in everything I do. She is my guardian angel, she is my reason to help others and she is my reason to become a better person and a better mum.

She is my Daughter, Lily

Nicky Whelan

Luke

It was an unseasonably warm, bright and beautiful April day. A spring day full of the promise of happiness, exciting changes and the end of a long wait for my first child, Luke. So I busied myself with preparations for his arrival. My hospital bag was already packed with a few carefully chosen outfits and essentials. I took the opportunity that such a warm day gave me, to potter around with my beloved horses, getting everything ready at the stables to hand over to a friend when Luke arrived.

I didn't notice at first that Luke wasn't moving. It was as I put my feet up in the evening that it dawned on me that I couldn't feel him kick, or remember when I had last felt him kick that day. So off we went to the hospital to make sure everything was alright. Once there I was scanned and was told the devastating news that Luke no longer had a heartbeat. That moment changed me and my life forever.

I spent two days waiting to meet Luke, and he was born at 2:40pm on 14th April 1997, at 36 weeks' gestation, weighing 5lb 10oz. He was just perfect, with lots of black hair and the cutest little button nose. I got to spend time with him in the hospital over the next few days, and that is time that I will always treasure. I was given his footprints and a lock of his gorgeous hair, and we took lots of photographs.

Tests showed that Luke wasn't poorly, and that I have a condition which causes me to have sticky blood, which made Luke gradually more sleepy until he gently passed away without any pain. Knowing Luke never felt poorly and did not suffer gives me great comfort.

I think about Luke every day. I miss him and long for him, but I do find that as the years pass it becomes a little easier. I thank Luke for showing me what matters in life, and for helping me appreciate the beauty around me and in my other children Sam and Jessica.

Luke has also brought me my wonderful 'Sands family', who mean so much to me. Together we have had so many adventures, in memory of Luke and all his angel friends. I send Luke love up to the sky every day, until we meet again.

Claire Cadman

Rosie

Rosie is our second beautiful daughter. She was born September 16th 2015 and passed away 28 hours later on September 17th. Rosie had Osteogenesis Imperfecta type 2.

We found out during the pregnancy that Rosie had severe problems with her bone growth. She had short long limbs and her chest was barrel shaped. They couldn't say for certain what was wrong but advised us to terminate the pregnancy which wasn't something I could do.

During my pregnancy with her big sister I'd dreamt that I had a baby girl born with short arms and legs. It was so surreal that it was the exact scenario happening.

We decided to give her every chance we could, and we were so grateful to have had those 28 amazing hours seeing her beautiful sparkly eyes and showering her with love.

Rosie Jo Tennick, our warrior princess, loved always, missed forever.

Joanne & Jonathan Tennick

Esmaé Amelia

Adam

Adam Bernard King

22/8/2010 the day my life changed forever. I was 9 days away from being started off but knew something wasn't right, a scan confirmed our baby's heart had stopped beating.

08:38 Sunday the 22/8/10 the exact time I felt my heart break and I knew I would never be the same again. Unless you have lost a baby you can only imagine what the pain is like. It changes everything in your life, how you look at life and the people around you. I felt different, alone, scared, damaged and broken.

Meeting Nicky and the rest of my amazing SANDS family changed that, they didn't fix it, but they made me see I can do this. Life will be different but I can be happy again and being part of this amazing dysfunctional family has made me happy again. Helping others is Adam's gift to me and for that I will be eternally grateful to my boy, Adam.

Emma Shepherd – Adams Mummy

Poppy

Poppy Grace Venables
1st November 2013

My husband and I had always wanted a big family. We were blessed in August 2009 with a bouncing baby boy George, followed 2 years later by our daughter Amelie. My third pregnancy was textbook. I practically sailed into the 3rd trimester without ever knowing anything was wrong, however the 30th October 2013 was the day that our entire world changed.

That day started out just like any other day, a bit of a mad rush to get our 4 year old to school on time so that I wouldn't be late to a midwife appointment at 9am (with our 22 month old in tow). But by 9:15 I knew something had gone terribly wrong with baby because the midwife couldn't find a heartbeat. She 'pretended' to blame her Doppler for playing up in an effort to stop me panicking, but in my heart I knew. My husband works in London so sadly he wasn't with me when it was confirmed at the hospital - that our beloved baby had died. At some point during the early hours that morning her heart had stopped beating.

I was sent home on pre-induction medication and had to endure a very traumatic Halloween at home in limbo, waiting to deliver. Even now, seeing Halloween things in the shops bring me out in a cold sweat, triggering so many emotions. Taking me back to those early, painful and isolating days.

On the 1st November, our beautiful daughter Poppy Grace Venables was born into deafening silence. Feelings of overwhelming love and utter despair in equal measure. I can't tell you how long I stared at her just willing her to breathe. So absolutely perfect in every way, we found out after her post mortem that it had 'most likely' been clotting inside my placenta that had caused her death. We were only able to spend 5 precious hours with her. How do you squeeze a lifetime of memories into 5 short hours? Our future without her seemed unfathomable. Words can't describe just how difficult it was to have to leave that hospital without our baby, only those who have walked in your shoes before truly know.

She was laid to rest in her forever bed on a very cold and frosty late November morning. I remember we had the first flurry of snow that day, the first sign of winter coming. It was raining and it felt like the sky was crying, just like me. At the closing of the service though the sun burst through the clouds and a sunbeam shone brightly through the stained glass window of the church and illuminated her in light. I was so thankful for that.

I am still learning how to live without her and some days are easier to bear than others. People say that time is a healer though I have yet to feel "healed". Most days start off the same; you wake up and for a few seconds everything is fine, and then you remember. And the sadness pours into your veins and feels like it is boiling hot and burning you. The constant guilt that when you laugh on the outside, you end up berating yourself for ever daring to feel happiness again. The guilt is always there. The should have, would have or could haves. The what ifs. The whys. Questions, so many questions… yet no answers will ever be enough. The emptiness. It throbs this pain, this love for your baby.

Sometimes it helps me to think of her running through a beautiful field of wildflowers and butterflies. I can picture her so vividly like this and the 3 year old I see before me is stunningly beautiful like her big sister, with a cheeky sparkle in her eyes just like her big brother. As she runs the wind whips her hair up behind her and it glistens in the sunlight like gold. Her fingers brush against dandelions and their seeds float up into the sky like fairies dancing. She's so full of life.

The heaven in my mind paints a comforting picture. She is wild and carefree. Some say that time in heaven might be compared to 'the blink of an eye' for us on this earth. I like that because it would mean that as she runs ahead of me, so happy and completely caught up in what she is doing, when she finally stops and looks behind her, I'll already be there.

Zoë and Steven Venables

Ruby

Lola

Declan – Nathaniel

An Angel in the book of life wrote down my baby's birth… then whispered as she closed the book… "Too Beautiful For Earth." – Author unknown

Declan – Nathaniel ♡
9th October 1994

Georgia – Lauren

An Angel in the book of life wrote down my baby's birth... then whispered as she closed the book... "Too Beautiful For Earth." – Author unknown

Georgia – Lauren ♡
1st August 1997

Nevaeh – Aaliyah

An Angel in the book of life wrote down my baby's birth… then whispered as she closed the book… "Too Beautiful For Earth." – Author unknown

Nevaeh – Aaliyah ♡
14th May 2014

Brogan

Archie

Archie Liam Hopkinson was born silent, but perfect, on the 4th July 2009, a day that broke my heart but I will forever treasure.

My delivery room was full, a senior midwife alongside normal midwives... they told me it looked like his heart rate had dropped just in the time it took to move me from one room to another. It was now 75 or 76 bmp... not good for the baby! They still never said anything in relation to what they thought it was. I had every faith he would be alright.

I remember them checking to see if I was bleeding. I remember nearly 'fainting' a few times and them telling me to stay with them. I remember the talk of an emergency section, also the anaesthetist sat talking me through a consent form.... no idea what she said but I signed. They checked again to see if I was dilating... no. Blood pressure check was normal! The consultant came in and kept questioning the heart rate. She insisted it must be mine but the senior midwife was saying very sternly "No, it is baby's." The next thing I knew I was being run down the corridor. I heard something crash on the floor and my midwife shouted "Whatever that was we are not stopping so get it and catch us up!"

The theatre staff started prepping, which panicked me because I was still awake! The iodine was on and everything. The woman who had the mask on my face then told me they couldn't do anything without her say so. It was just 3 minutes of pure oxygen I was having at that point... just 3 minutes... that 3 minutes could have probably saved him...Then nothing...

I remember coming round slightly and my eyes were still closed and asking where Chris was and while she was answering that question the penny dropped, I had just had my son! So the next question was asked, "Where is my baby? Where is Archie?" I still had my eyes closed at this point still very fuzzy headed, groggy, still coming round...I sensed some hesitation.... so I instantly knew at that point something was not right so I was trying to get off the bed! They made me lay back down and put my legs back on the bed.

I don't remember if I was in pain.... then someone said those words, those words that no one should hear.... "I am so sorry we did everything we could....." I rolled onto my side (the best I could) and sobbed. Then Chris appeared. They took me back onto delivery where I was insisting they bring my baby now. Because of how I was reacting in theatre it was the staff in there that had to tell me. Normally the senior midwife did that. The senior midwife went to get Archie. I remember them handing me my baby and I took in this big breath and sobbed because I couldn't believe how perfect he was and how much he looked like he was asleep.

The midwife I had for the day was fantastic. They did his foot prints, hand prints, a lock of his hair, photos etc. then asked if we wanted him dressing. I said "Yes but I want to see his bum before you put his nappy on."

When she dressed him, she handed my baby back to me. I was still a proud mum, I still wanted to show him off but I didn't know what was normal. I was in a far from normal situation. What did other people do? When my midwife mentioned photos I was a bit surprised. I don't know why, I suppose it just didn't seem right, but it was more than alright. The hospital took some photos. We had some taken with him and to look at them breaks my heart. They printed one each for our other children, I thought that was lovely!

While I laid there feeling like my heart was so heavy I felt so detached from everyone, like I was watching all this going on around me, like I was watching someone else's life go so terribly wrong. Would I ever feel normal again? Did I even want to feel normal again? What exactly was normal now? I knew he was gone but he was still my boy, still mummy's little Prince. You see it on films where something terrible happens and they have that sob which sticks in their throat... well I suppose I never thought it actually happens until that Saturday.

Visitors came and went, each one offering condolences. I lay in that bed unable to move, unable to think of anything other than 'that's my baby'. Yet I still felt sorry for each one of my visitors, each visitor that came and sat with tears in their eyes as they held Archie. I was the one apologising for them being upset. I felt bad that I had done this; I had caused so many tears. I felt for each one for different reasons. Chris mainly because he had lost his son and watching me grieve like he had never seen before.

Our other children arrived to meet their long awaited baby brother. Even though they knew what had happened they still came in with their faces lit up. My heart broke all over again! They looked so proud, so happy. I knew they would need me at home but I knew they were well looked after with my sisters. All I could think about was this is my time for Archie, I won't get another chance but the girls have me forever (Selfish, I know).

Photos were being taken, people coming and going, different midwives coming in to see him and saying sorry.

Questions, questions, questions! Those questions you don't want to think about, those you never in your wildest dreams you never thought you would be asked... "Have you thought about the funeral?"

All I kept thinking was "NO! I don't want to think about it! How do you choose whether to bury or cremate your baby?" I knew what both involved! I didn't want either. I just wanted to take him home, home where he belonged.

When it was Chris, myself and our son, just us three, the room was so unnaturally quiet. I couldn't take my eyes off our baby, so perfect. I watched for a flicker, a twitch. Maybe they were wrong. Of course deep down I knew I wasn't going to see any movements. I watched for his chest moving... nothing... nothing but a peaceful looking baby laid in my arms and in Chris's.

Through the night I held Archie on my chest where I could keep him warm, stroke his cheek and kiss his forehead. I didn't want to let him go.

Archie died due to a concealed abruption.

Seven years on Archie remains a big part of our lives. His name travels all over the world with friends and even strangers. They write his name on paper or in sand then they send me the photos via Facebook which I print and keep in an album. His name has been in all 50 states of America. He's had his name with Mickey Mouse in Florida. His memory will live on through us and others.

Loved, missed, treasured.

Louise and Chris Hopkinson

Ashley Dean

To my darling Ashley.

I couldn't believe that you had gone
But in my heart you still live on
I never held you in my arms
You were born fast asleep
I never held your tiny hand
You were never mine to keep.

My little boy you are always here
Nearly every day I shed a tear,
Every day you are never more than a thought away.
In my mind your little face I see
That little nose, those rosebud lips
A perfect picture of your face.

They say time heals everything
I know this isn't true,
Because it hurts so much today
As the day I lost you.

The tiny babe never laid in my arms
I can't even picture this
I could never on your cheek
Place a tiny kiss.

The tears that flow fill buckets,
Oh how life's unfair
I wish that that just once
I could have stroked your downy hair.

And in my nose that baby smell,
Just once oh just once please
But this will never happen
And life makes no guarantees.

I feel the anger once again,
Why did it have to be you?
Sometimes when I think of it,
It seems so untrue.

I wish the clock could rewind just to the day before
Then I could tell the doctors what I know now
It was a twisted cord suffocating you
Before you were born.

I know how stupid this may sound,
But if only it could come true
Sadly Ashley it never will
So I send all my love to you.

The one I love is with you Mum
Please hug and hold him for me
Keep him safe in your arms
Until I can come up to see

Then I will wrap my arms around him
And never let him go
Until that time I will think of you
And in the wind lots of kisses to you I'll blow

For the baby son I loved and wanted so much but lost.
Love you forever my darling son may you know that one of
my greatest blessings was having you.

Love Mum xxxxxx

Ashley Dean Hopkinson
Born Asleep 11th September 1970

Kristine Holmes

Theo

Theo was stillborn at 25 weeks on Friday 30th May 2014 at 16:55. Theo had already died before I went into labour. We do not know why our little boy died or what caused his heart to stop beating.

Chesterfield SANDS have provided me with light in the dark days, weeks, months and now years since Theo grew his angel wings. It is through Chesterfield SANDS that I met my lovely friend Nicola. Our little boys due dates were very close. They are both called Theo and have very similar surnames. I like to think of them playing together in the clouds above.

It is important to me that our babies are remembered through different events to raise money for Sands and to support other families. Sadly, the people who best understand the heartbreak of stillbirth are those that have experienced it themselves.

Louisa

Phoenix James

Violet

Lucy

Lucy Mabel Roberts

"Each new life, no matter how brief, forever changes the world."
Author Unknown

Twinkle, twinkle little star,
Do you know how loved you are?
Author Unknown

Saturday 30th August

My mummy's waters broke at 5:30am, ten days after I was due to come into the world. I think my big sister must have known something, because she woke up shortly afterwards. My mummy went into labour almost straight away, with the contractions being just a few minutes apart.

My mummy phoned the hospital and we were asked to go in to be assessed. When we got there we had all the checks and everything was fine, but it turned out that I had done a poo already! I just had to have my heart rate monitored, to check that I wasn't getting upset.

We moved down to the labour ward and at about half past eleven I was about ready to be born. I came into the world absolutely perfect at 12:04pm. My mummy and daddy thought I was so perfect and beautiful. It didn't take long before I cried and proved I had got a good set of lungs. I scored well on my tests too. 7/10 on the Apgar scale after 1 minute and then 10/10 after 5 minutes.

My daddy had lots of cuddles while the midwife checked my mummy over. I opened my eyes briefly and sucked my thumb too. I then got to have some cuddles with my mummy.

After just a few hours we were moved up to the ward and I had a little drink of my mummy's milk. I then started to get a bit cold, so I had a cuddle with my mummy again.

The nurse then thought I should be getting a bit warmer, so she put me under a cosy heat lamp. Unfortunately that didn't seem to work and then I started to get a bit more poorly. I had a bit of a dusky episode, so the nurse asked for some doctors to come and look at me.

The doctors came very quickly, at about 5:30pm. They thought that I might have a bit of an infection, due to the fact that I had pooed earlier before I was born. I was whisked down to the Neonatal unit, so that they could find out what the matter was.

I had lots of tests. They looked at my heart, my lungs and my blood, but they couldn't really find anything wrong with me. It was the first time I had been without my mummy. My mummy and daddy had to wait three hours before they could come and see me. They were very worried.

At 9:00pm they were asked to come to the Neonatal unit. I was rigged up to machines to check my heart rate and breathing. They were all fine. The doctors still didn't know what was the matter with me, but they thought I might have been having some seizures. I became more poorly and at 12:00am I was finding it difficult to breath and sometimes I would just stop, so the doctors decided to ventilate me. I had to have lots of drugs to make my body relax more.

Sunday 31st August

My mummy and daddy were ever so worried. They were shown to a little quiet room where they could wait while the doctors did more tests. The doctors were concerned as they still were not sure what was the matter. They told my mummy and daddy that I might have a poorly brain. I was very sleepy, partly because of the drugs, and partly because of being poorly. My head was rigged to an ECG screen to check what my brain might be doing.

Mummy and daddy stayed with me most of the night, watching my machines and hoping that I would come round quickly. In the morning the doctors were more concerned and didn't seem to think that I had an infection. They thought that it might be better if I were to be transferred to Jessop Hospital in Sheffield where there are some really good baby doctors.

A special ambulance came for me and the doctors and nurses got me all ready for my first journey on the road. I had to be in a special incubator, with my own oxygen and seat belts. My mummy wasn't allowed with me in case she got poorly, as it wasn't long since she had given birth to me.

The journey went very well and I arrived at my new hospital. I had a new incubator and I was in a room with three other babies.

My mummy and daddy got there very quickly too and were given a room at the hospital so they could stay and visit me anytime.

The doctors were still not sure what was wrong with me, but planned to do a lot more testing and they gave me more medicines to treat all kinds of illnesses that I might have.

My mummy kept expressing milk for me, as she wanted to be able to do what she could for me and to be able to breast feed me when I got better. The doctors and nurses kept explaining what they were going to do and what might be wrong with me, but I still wasn't getting any better. I was still very sleepy and needed the machine to help me breath.

All through the night mummy and daddy kept checking on me. They were very worried and sad.

Monday 1st September

Early Monday morning, my mummy came to visit me. I enjoyed her stroking me and even wriggled a little when she tickled me. I sometimes even did little movements by myself. My mummy thought I might be a little bit better. She kept looking at my ECG machine hoping that the little brain waves on there were showing some promise.

I saw another very good doctor on the Monday morning. He did a little scan of my brain and explained to mummy and daddy that he thought I may have had a stroke. He needed to know more about what had happened inside my brain, so decided to send me for a CAT scan. I had my second ambulance journey, but this time it wasn't far at all – just to

Sheffield Children's Hospital across the road. My mummy was allowed to come too. It didn't take long to do the scan. When my mummy looked at the man's face after the scan, there was no smile, just sadness in his eyes.

Later that day I had lots of visitors, my nana and granddad came to the hospital along with my big sister and my uncle. All the grownups came to meet me.

In the afternoon, the consultant came to talk to my mummy and daddy. He took them to a pretty, quiet room along with two other doctors. My mummy and daddy had a bad feeling about what he was going to say. He explained that I had experienced a catastrophic stroke from which I could not get better. He explained that he didn't know when it had happened, or why, and that it was very unusual to happen after I had been so well.

My mummy and daddy were very sad, but relieved that they knew what was the matter with me. They were happy that I didn't have to have any more tests or drugs, as it made them feel upset to know what I had already been through in my short little life. They understood that they would only have one more day with me.

Late that evening, they were able to help the nurses look after me. They were able to change my nappy and give me lots of cuddles. It was lovely to feel my mummy and daddy close to me and hear their voices again. They sat with me for ages.

Tuesday 2nd September

The next day was a busy day for me. Firstly, I got to have some cuddles with nana and granddad and my uncle. They were pleased to hold me, but they were sad too. Then my grandma and granddad came and held me too. Finally I got to meet my big sister Alice. She was very excited to see me and kept smiling and pointing at me. My mummy and daddy were able to give me more cuddles too.

In the afternoon we all moved to the quiet room. A chaplain came and said some nice words and baptised me, and my big sister Alice sprinkled water on my head! My mummy and daddy had thought long and hard about my name;

Lucy: *meaning light*
Mabel: *meaning beautiful and beloved*
Roberts: *my daddy's and sister's name*

It was then time for the rest of my family to go home. My mummy and daddy wanted some time alone with me. They were able to have lots more cuddles with me. They made lots of memories with me too. They printed my hands and feet, cut lockets of my hair and took lots of photos of me. They wanted to be able to remember me in as many ways as possible.

Sadly it was then time to say goodbye. When my breathing machine was turned off I peacefully slipped away. My heart was very strong though and kept beating for a long time. The whole time my daddy held me in his arms, he told me that mummy and daddy loved me very much and I wasn't to be frightened.

I died at 6:30pm

The hospital still had no idea what had caused the stroke after Lucy had been born so well. They suggested a post mortem be carried out. As Lucy's case was so unusual this was done at Great Ormond Street Hospital by one of their top experts in this area. Sadly only possible explanations were provided and the exact cause of what happened to Lucy will always be unknown.

We think of Lucy every day, remember how perfect she was, and always will be, and miss her in our lives immensely. Lucy will never be forgotten.

We love you Lucy xxx

Twinkle, Twinkle Little Star
May you always know how special you are.
Author Unknown

xxxxxxxxxxxx Sweet dreams little baby girl xxxxxxxxxxxx

Lee and Amy.

Jak and Harrison

We are the proud parents to 2 angel boys who we miss with all of our being each and every day.

On the 3rd of December 2004 our son Jak Jay was kicking furiously in my tummy. We were laughing at how crazy he was being. The next day I felt no movement. Friends said it's because I was 37 wks and he was settling ready to be born.

The next day was a Sunday and Jay was doing overtime at work. He rang and I said I'd still not felt him move. He could sense the worry in my voice so came home and we went to our maternity unit. They knew us well as I had polyhydramnios and had been under a lot of supervision, in and out of hospital for the last couple of months.

Sadly that afternoon we learned that our son at 37wks of pregnancy had no heartbeat and we would have to give birth to him. I was sent home for 2 long days waiting for tablets to soften my cervix to aid induction. Tuesday the 7th of December at 4.58pm Jak Jay was born silently weighing 8lb 11oz. The only notable cause of death was cord accident. Obviously on the Friday evening he had gotten wrapped in his cord and the kicking was him fighting to live.

Eleven months later I was 33 wks pregnant with another boy, we had named him Harrison. Again I had polyhydramnios which is too much amniotic fluid. The hospital was constantly monitoring me and at my last scan on the Monday, Harrison was in the breach position. On Thursday he turned; an uncomfortable feeling to say the least. He didn't move again and I just knew he had died. 2 days later my worst fears were realised and in hospital it was confirmed he had no heartbeat.

2 days later on 14th November 2005 I gave birth to a 7lb beautiful boy.

Our angels play together in a world of rainbows and sparkles forever more.

Jay & Julie Cooke

Archie

Raife

David Ezra

Leigha-Jade and Amiee-Grace

Leigha-Jade Larner-Newton

On the 22nd of December 2011 my life changed. When I found out I was going to be a mummy again I was over the moon. Another baby brother or sister for my first born Lexi-Mae. My antenatal appointments were going to plan till I had my blood test done for the Downs screening. I remember very clearly that day, the midwife knocking on my door to say that I was high risk and to book an appointment at the hospital for more tests. I was on edge and wanted to know what was wrong with my baby.

Me and my partner decided to book a private scan at Sheffield. Suddenly I felt like something wasn't quite right. I also remember this day as clear as anything. My partner and my mum came along to the private scan. We were finally going to find out the sex of our baby. We sat in the waiting room.

The sonographer shouted my name and we went in. I lay there on the couch with my little bump hanging out. I told the lady why I wanted the scan (high risk for Downs Syndrome). She began to scan my bump. The look on her face said it all, I knew then something wasn't right.

She told me she didn't like the look of my scan and told me that my poor baby had not properly formed. My whole world was broken. I lay there sobbing with my mum and partner holding my hand. The lady told me that my poor baby was a little girl. She carried on scanning after I calmed down. I left the room with my heart sinking. My poor baby, what was I going to do? My whole life was shattered.

As I remember I rang the hospital at Chesterfield to be told to go for another scan. I told the midwife what the sonographer had found. She began to scan me and told me that she would like me to attend Sheffield for a scan. My whole world shattered as I got told to sit and wait while the midwife rang Jessops Hospital as they have consultants who are more specialised.

The next day I went to Jessops. There I was again, with my bump, having another scan. The doctor told me that my baby girl was very poorly and that my little girl's chance of living would be minimal. My precious baby had broken bones inside me. How could she?

I had MRI scans which gave false hope. I remember a specialist coming to talk to me about my little girls bones but they didn't come to see me till quiet far along in my pregnancy. They told me she had osteogenesis imperfecta type 2 and they wanted me to put my little girl to sleep. I just couldn't do it.

I gave my little girl every chance a mum would. She was born on the 22/12/2011 by emergency C-section and weighed 3lb 5oz. We called her Leigha-Jade Larner-Newton. As I watched them try do everything they could for my baby girl, they couldn't save her as she was so poorly, I just wanted to hold her. I remember shouting for my baby.

The lady passed her to her daddy as I was laid on the theatre table. I held her near me with her cheek on mine. I told her I loved her and always will and I was sorry I couldn't help her.

I put my hand on her chest. I could feel her heartbeat getting weaker. She sadly fell to sleep 20 minutes after being born.

The pain I felt, watching my own baby slip away. There is always a piece of my heart missing.

My heart will miss you every day and you are always and forever in my heart.

Love you always.

Mummy and Daddy xx

Amiee-Grace Larner-Newton

On the 13.08.2012, the week before my 21st birthday, I lost my second angel due to a miscarriage, even though I was a day off being 9 weeks, my hopes and dreams came crashing down before me.

Not only did we lose our first angel the year before, but I had to go through a miscarriage too. My heart was broken again another piece of my heart missing. I started to wonder why. Why me? Have I not suffered enough?

After tests we found out our baby was a girl and she had Turners Syndrome. I called our baby Amiee-Grace. My babies had 2 totally different things wrong. I couldn't get my head round it. Apparently it was just a mistake in a gene. Like my first angel there was no explanation why this happened. We went through genetic tests but they told us nothing as they came back ok.

I suppose we will never get the answers as to why it happened. I never got to hold and cuddle her. I never got to see who she looked like, but I will hold her in my heart always. She was still my baby and will always be missed.

Mummy and Daddy love you always xx

Kaylie Larner-Newton & Phil Newton

Mummy and Daddy to two Angels

James

My son James Andrew Bailey-Fryer was stillborn on 21st November 2011 at Derby Royal Hospital. The most beautiful little boy I'd laid eyes on and the most heart-breaking time of my life.

I don't remember much apart from being in a beautiful room called the butterfly suite, designed for parents that have to endure this terrible time. The room was calming with a little court yard. When the finally brought him to me, all dressed in white, in a tiny little Moses basket, it was like he was just sleeping. I was handed a memory box made by the donations people give to SANDS. That memory box gave me comfort and is to this day a very important part of our lives.

I gave back to SANDS after that by doing a fun run with my daughter Laila-Grace. She was 3 at the time but ran half the 2k with me and the rest on my back. £350 we managed to raise! For all the hard work that SANDS do, I wanted to give that little back.

Kelly Bailey
Age 34 from Ripley, Derbyshire

Riley Lomas

On the 5th July at 10.24am our darling Riley came into the world, a massive 14 weeks early. He was so tiny weighing just 1lb4.8oz. Daddy got a quick glance at him when he was born, but it was to be a whole 5 hours till I finally set eyes on my beautiful baby boy.

He was gorgeous. Words cannot describe how lucky we felt. We would sit for hours just looking over him in his incubator. His little hands would clutch tightly around my little finger. I remember the day he opened his eyes for the first time. I was ecstatic! We just looked at each other for ages and I told him I was his mummy. I couldn't wait for the day we could hold him properly.

We had to wait 4 weeks for this and they got me a nursing chair to sit on comfortably and they placed him on me and I just cried. He was so content just lying against my chest. I felt bad as daddy was at work, but I couldn't wait a moment longer the minute they said I could hold him. When daddy finally got to hold him, Riley had very bad wind and wouldn't stop trumping on him. It was really funny.

Riley was a feisty little boy and he didn't like being prodded and poked too much, but I couldn't help but touch him. He had my little nose and his daddy's long legs and big feet. Like most babies he really disliked having his nappy changed. He would wriggle his little legs around in protest, getting his feet all in a mess so I would have to clean those too.

These are just a few of the many precious memories that we have of Riley, we'd be here all day if I was to share them all.

In loving memory of Riley Ashton Lomas
05/07/2016-23/08/2016

Mummy and Daddy miss you so much and you're forever in
our hearts xxxxx

Claire Blackbourn & Adam Lomas

10 small fingers, 10 tiny toes
2 long legs and a cute button nose
Blonde tufts of hair, a perfect little face
Your beautiful baby Riley will never be replaced

7 short weeks just 49 days
You watched over him with a loving gaze
The few times his little body you were able to hold
Those memories will stay forever
More precious than diamonds or gold

Your special little boy so sadly taken away
You have cried so many tears praying he would stay
Those stars will shine extra bright up in the sky above
For they have gained an angel
Whose short life was full of love

I hope one day I will not cry because you have gone but I will
smile and be happy because you are my special little one'

Sally Collins

Kian

Sam

Joe

Ian

In 1967, I was aged six, my mother had just given birth to my baby brother and everything was just perfect. Three weeks later my world was turned upside down with very little understanding or explanation about what had happened.

I was woken up by my Dad and brother going out in the car. I jumped out of bed and ran into Mum and Dads bedroom to find where Mum was. Only Ian was there, in his cot, very quiet and not moving.

After giving him a little shake there was no response so I ran down stairs to find Mum. I asked her about Ian. She said he was dead and had died in the night. She told me to get dressed and go out and play.

No more was mentioned about Ian until the day of his funeral. We were not going to attend, but to go to school as usual and a neighbour would look after us till Mum and Dad came home.

Since nothing was ever explained to me I thought Ian had been put in the loft and if I came out my room at night he would jump down on me. This thought scared me and stayed with me for many years.

As time went by Ian was never spoken about. Never once was his birthday ever remembered. The only time my father spoke about Ian was when my mother passed away unexpectedly. He arranged for her ashes to be scattered with Ian's in the same crematorium garden.

Thankfully things have improved over the years and baby loss is spoken about and the support group SANDS do a fantastic job with the parents, helping them to cope with grief and allowing these babies to have a voice.

Ann Smith

Austyn

The morning of 17th January 2012 I'm at work and I get the call…..she's got pains, we need to go to the hospital. I leave work, shout and scream to my workmates with excitement, I'M GONNA BE A DADDY!!!!!!!!!

Driving home I'm full of emotions from joy to pride to fear. I get home, rush Mandy into the car and we're off, both buzzing with excitement. "Lex!" she says "my waters have broke", but when she feels there's blood….. My heart sinks …what's happened?…..This is bad!……How's Mandy?..... How's my boy? All these things rushing through my head, but I can't let her know I'm scared. "Its fine honey, just a show" I say whilst secretly speeding up to get to the hospital a.s.a.p.

The next ten mins is a blur until we get in the room and Mandy is on a bed. There's nurse's running around everywhere, monitors on her belly, machines beeping. This is it, Austyn is coming!

I hold Mandy's hand and she squeezes my hand so tight and with tears in her eyes says "what's happening is everything ok?"

"Its fine" I say. "We're here now, not long and we'll be mummy and daddy. I love you" I say and kiss her on the head.

More frantic rushing around by doctors and nurses and then we're rushed into another room with nurses saying everything is fine, it's just checks. But in my mind I know something is wrong… but I'm the MAN!.... I can't be scared… I need to be strong for Mandy.

What seems like hours pass until the doctor comes in (I think it was maybe a minute). They look at the monitors and I can see in their eyes what is happening. I squeeze Mandy's hand with tears in my eyes, and then it came, those words, "there's no heartbeat."

My whole life collapsed around me, everything I have wanted, all my life taken away with 3 words. How can this happen to us, what have we done? We're good people…. We don't want much…. just a family. I look at Mandy and realise she needs me to be strong. I grab her and we squeeze and cry and scream but all is quiet, nothing can get through to me, I'm numb!

Now we have decisions to make. Do we have a C-section, does she go through labour.

Mandy can't go through labour so she has the C-section. I have never wanted to not leave her as much as this, she needs me! But I have to let her go. I reassure her and say "I'll see you later with our boy. I love you."

Whilst she's gone I get taken to a quiet room where I can phone and tell the family about the tragedy. When I walk into the room, finally I'm alone. I can break down, no one can see me. I'm not letting anyone down. I cry so hard. But I have to stop and pull myself together.

12:50 we are in the family room surrounded by close family and the nurse comes in with a sombre smile and says "He's here, you can see him." When I walk in he's there, my gorgeous little man, so perfect in every way. I walk over and just want him to cry, but he's silent. I ask to hold him.

The nurse leaves us for a while and I talk to him. I don't cry because he is my boy, my pride and joy. I can't take my eyes of him or stop kissing him. What a miracle he is. We weigh him, get him dressed and walk through the corridor to the family room as proud as punch that I am a daddy.

When the door opens and they see him we cry together and they ask to hold him. It's a great time, but the saddest time of my life. All the time I'm still scared for Mandy. HOW IS SHE!? I pick up my son and walk to show him the world through the window. As I open the window the sun shines on his little head and I tell him about his mother and ask him to be strong for her and keep her safe.

Finally the nurses say Mandy is ok and she's in the recovery room so I can see her and show her our son. But then the nurse says Mandy is very delicate. She's had to have a blood transfusion and we nearly lost her. When I see her face, it's like she's not there. She looks at me and I say hello mummy and pass Austyn to her. Her face lights up as she sees how perfect he is.

I ask the doctor what happened in surgery and they say that it was a close run thing and that Mandy had suffered a placenta abruption. She had lost so much blood during this that I wouldn't have been leaving with both of them whatever would have happened...... my boy had given up his life for his mummy, my already perfect miracle little boy is now also my hero!

That night we stay in hospital and we keep Austyn with us and cuddle and kiss him, dress him in so many outfits, ha ha and just enjoy having our little man with us for as long as we can. The next two nights we stay in hospital and Mandy is nursed back to health and we have Austyn with us as much as we can.

Austyn Alexei Ian Robinson was born at 12:48 17th January 2012 and I will treasure the short time I had with him for the rest of my life. I always search for the little things to keep him here and to make me feel that he is still here with me. One of those things is that on that day at 13:00 a horse called Lexi's boy ran its debut race and won. This is the same time I was alone with Austyn... My boy... Lexi's boy. Some people may find this silly but it's the silly things that get you through.

I wanted to share my story with dads everywhere that have been through this terrible thing, to let them know that you can cry; you can break down. It's not a bad thing and you are no less of a man. We all have our male bravado but we also all need help sometimes. Do your grieving and have a break-down whenever or however you can. I used to do it alone, walking in the hills with the dog, but that's just my way. Dads go through it too. It's not that people forget us, it's just we don't ask for the help when we need it.
Me and my now wife Mandy talk about Austyn every day and we have been blessed with a daughter Amelia who we tell about Austyn, her brother, all the time. Thank you for reading my story and I hope it helps in some way. It's really helped me to get this out as I have never spoken about it in this much detail, so thank you again for reading.

Thanks.

Alexei Robinson.

Mia

Elsa Jane

Casey-Leigh

Jassy

Nathaniel

Teegan

29th April 2012 was just another normal day at work. My first pregnancy, so I was feeling the tiredness a little extra from my 6am shift start. Having my first bundle of joy on the way, I wanted to get as many extra shifts as possible in, so I worked straight through till dinner.

Back home for my lunch I even remember making a corned beef toastie and a cuppa and sitting to watch the secret garden on tele and quickly drifted off. I couldn't have been asleep that long when I woke to a sharp sudden pain in my stomach: I knew something was wrong.

I rung my mum who just instructed me to take some paracetamol and it's just my body preparing for baby. As I prepared to get up I just remember going dizzy and waking up to my mum and a paramedic.

I sadly don't remember much between then and getting to Jessops Maternity Unit, but apparently I was sent to Chesterfield Royal Hospital and within half an hour my mum said I was transferred on blue lights.

The next few days were a blur of nurses and being injected with pain relief and steroids. My mum informed me after it was a serious case of pre-eclampsia and it was me or baby.

2nd May 2012 at 2.10am after 13 hours of labour Teegan Louise Woods arrived - stillborn.

It's strange what people remember of certain occasions and sadly I don't remember as much as I'd like, but she will forever be remembered as my first born. *My heartbeat is your lullaby* ♡

Gemma - Mummy to an Angel X

Kiara

Isla

Danita Jay

Baby Servante

Joshua

Benjamin – John

Jacob

Jacob Joshua James O'Connor

Our baby boy Jacob was born on the 31st of May 2015 by Emergency C-Section.
He was 40 weeks + 2 days gestation.

My waters had broken on the 30th. We went to the hospital to be checked. Everything looked fine so I was sent home to let the labour progress.

In the early hours of the 31st I had found meconium, therefore we phoned the hospital and they asked for us to come in. When I got there they checked me over. Jacob's heart rate was very low. By the time they delivered him, it was too late. Our precious boy passed away 12 hours later.

We haven't been given a reason to why it happened just it's one of those things.

We miss him every day, Think of him every day, wonder how he'd look now, how much he'd have grown and what kind of personality he'd have. We cannot help wondering what age he would have been when reaching milestones compared to his baby brother.

We love you so much Jacob. Thank you for the time we had with you. You made your family bigger and stronger.

Twinkle twinkle little star, mummy and daddy love you, however far, you are.

Xxxx

Kerry Baines and Joshua O'Connor

Charlie

Charlie's story, I think, will be very different to the others you might read here. In fact, there's a part of me which always feels like I'm some kind of fraud, and that our tale doesn't quite belong here. It's a long one, and there is quite a lot of background. I hope you will stick with it though, because it's the background which makes up a big part of the story. Every life is precious though, no matter how small or insignificant and Charlie was certainly precious to us in many ways.

Rob and I got together when we were 17, moved in together at 22 and married at 24. Like a lot of people, our priority was to build a home and be financially stable before starting a family. Our focus was our different careers, enjoying travelling and I guess enjoying our life. At 27 we decided we finally felt ready to start a family. Month after month passed by - no pregnancy. Months turned into years. Every month getting our hopes built up, just for them to be dashed. I became slightly obsessed, and tried anything possible. I spent a fortune on ovulation testing kits, monitored my basal body temperature amongst other crazy things. After two years we finally went to see our GP who arranged for a number of different, painful and embarrassing tests before referring us to a fertility specialist at the local general hospital. The results already suggested there were potential infertility issues on both sides. Having a child of our own felt completely out of reach. Being able to conceive a child was supposed to be the easiest and most natural thing in the world, but it wasn't to us. I felt inadequate as a woman, like there must be something wrong with me, and I think Rob also felt like he was responsible.

The consultant we were referred to pretty much confirmed our worst fears. Our issues made it highly unlikely we would ever be able to conceive naturally and our best chance would be IVF treatment, with ICSI. I won't bore you too much with the science, but basically the best quality sperm would literally be injected into the egg in a petri dish. If an embryo developed then it would be inserted back into the womb. As neither of us had children, and there was no treatment which could help either of our conditions, we were offered funding through the NHS for one full, fresh cycle.

We had a few weeks to decide if we wanted to go ahead, and also choose a clinic we wanted to go to. At the time I thought it was one of the hardest decisions I had to make. Personally, I'm terrified of needles and all sorts of chemicals and artificial hormones would be stuffed into me. They'd give me drugs to stop my natural cycle, then drugs to simulate my eggs to grow and multiply (and grow so much that at a certain point in the cycle you are not allowed to do anything strenuous as your ovaries are so swollen they could burst), drugs to thicken and maintain the lining of the room. The only way I can describe it is having your normal monthly cycle but on an extreme level, and hormones don't just affect the physical, they affect your emotions too as I'm sure most women will testify. Plus the whole cycle is an emotional rollercoaster in itself, which only actually carried a 30% chance of getting pregnant, depending on how your body responds to the treatment. You make it through several different hurdles during the cycles and while the drugs can do a lot, nothing can be done to make the egg and the sperm develop into embryos, or for an embryo to actually implant in the womb. That was out of everyone's hands, even the specialists.

I had so many concerns, not only just around the physical things, but also ethically and morally which we discussed over and over between us.

A month or two later we eventually decided to sign our fate to science. It felt like a brave and bold decision, but deep down I was actually terrified. We began the process towards the end of May 2013 and I never thought we would be successful. Would we make it through every stage? The daily injections took affect and my ovaries responded, the scans eventually showing 18 eggs that were developing. My lining was also getting thick, and a date was scheduled for collection. Out of those 18, 11 were good enough to be fertilised. Eight of those actually fertilised. Six made it to day two. The clinic were still hopeful for a day five transfer (a five day embryo is called a Blastocyst, and they have a greater chance of implanting in the womb). Day three we just had four left, and on day four we had three. The clinic would call us in the morning to say if any of the remaining three embryos would be good enough to implant.

That morning was tough. We both went to work as normal, but had booked the afternoon off work if it was needed. We were on tenterhooks just waiting for that call. It eventually came at about 10.30am. Two embryos had survived. We were going ahead with the transfer of what looked to be the best quality blastocyst, and they would freeze the other with our permission should we want them to.

We got to see our blastie on the screen before it went in. It just looked like a blob, but it was our blob and I think I fell in love instantly with that cell on the screen. I took a photo of it on my phone. The transfer itself didn't go entirely smoothly. Apparently my cervix has a funny bend which they hadn't been prepared to navigate around. At one point the embryologist told them to stop because our blastie had been out of the incubator too long. We paused for 10 minutes and then started again. Eventually it made it in, and now my job was to give this blastie the best home possible for the next 14 days and just hope.

The clinic sent us home with a pregnancy test kit and a number to call with my test result. Those two weeks dragged on and on and on. I was following everything to the letter and trying not to read anything into any symptom because I was still well aware that anything could go wrong and there were no guarantees.

We woke at 5am on test day, feeling both nervous and excited. Our wait was over. I went off to do the test while Rob waited in the next room. The line appeared almost instantly, but I wasn't sure if I was actually pregnant or seeing things. I ran in to show him the test, and he looked and looked before finally confirming what I thought. I was pregnant! I squealed and jumped up and down and Rob hugged me tight. We'd made it, I was finally pregnant! Not quite believing it, I went out to the supermarket and bought several more tests, including a digital one, all of which said I was pregnant!

The next stage was to go for a scan after two weeks where they would check the pregnancy was developing. I was using pessaries daily, which contain a hormone which would actually give you the symptoms of pregnancy anyway. I'd have to use them until about 13 weeks, gradually reducing them, but that is why they schedule in for early scans. We were so happy to be expecting, all our friends and family knew what was happening. I'd been open at work because of all the appointments I'd needed, and it made no sense to keep the news away from people being as they knew we had been going through IVF anyway.

Week six- it was July 23 and Rob's 30th birthday. There on the scan was a tiny little blobby embryo, tucked neatly in to my womb. Inside that embryo was the tinniest beating heart. We watched it in fascination, flickering away. Its heartbeat had been so easy for the sonographer to find. It was my baby, and it was growing inside of me. I felt so happy. There was just one thing. She had spotted a small haematoma in my womb, and it looked like it could be nothing, possibly just bruising from the difficult transfer but she would like us to come back in two weeks for another scan to check everything was ok.

I did hear that. I really did hear the bit about the haematoma, but I guess I was just so over the moon that I didn't quite think about it enough.

Week eight- August 5. I returned for another scan, this time with my mum because Rob had been called to jury duty which there was no getting out of. I was excited to be bringing my mum along to share this experience with me. While we were sat waiting, I talked to her about our frozen embryo, who was right here in this building, and a little brother or sister to the one growing inside my tummy. I was so used to coming to the clinic now, and I was so used to scans. The sonographer was very quiet though, and unlike other times she didn't immediately turn the screen to show me my baby. She said she just needed to get the consultant to check something. The consultant came into the room and continued with the scan. After a few seconds he stopped and told me the devastating news that our baby had died. There was no longer a beating heart.

They took us into a room. One of the rooms where you sit and wait before a procedure. I called Rob to tell him the news. And I cried. And cried. The next step was to stop taking the pessaries to allow the baby to pass out of my body naturally. They arranged an appointment for me to return in two weeks so they could check how things were.

I struggle to write here to express just how I felt over the next two weeks. I felt like a walking coffin, like someone had written a symbol of death on me. I stopped crying, and everyone else took over. Everyone cried. I felt numb. Disbelief I googled and googled to see if they could be wrong, but I knew they were not wrong. Blame. I went through everything

I had done in the past two weeks that could have caused my baby to die. I found several things I thought I'd done- even eating smoked salmon. I didn't eat. I barely ate anything for days. I had to punish myself. This was my fault, I couldn't do the one thing I was supposed to do as a woman. I didn't sleep. Instead of sleeping I found a dark place where I considered different ways to end my life, reading through forums where people shared their failed suicide attempts and discussed how not to make the same mistake next time. There were people offering to sell you arsenic. But that wasn't right for me. I couldn't do that because I didn't want it to go wrong. I came to the conclusion that the best thing I could do would be to drive out of Derbyshire to a big cliff and drive my car off the top of it.

People sent me flowers. People told me that it happened all the time and I could try again. People said god had done the kindest thing because the baby must have had something horribly wrong with it and it would never have survived. Some people just couldn't talk to me at all. Some people didn't want to talk about it - you don't speak of these things.

Still no miscarriage though. No bleeding, nothing until the night before I was due to go back for the scan, and it was horrendous. We cried. Rob more than me because he felt powerless. It was over.

Week ten- We went to our scan and I described the blood loss and tissue loss to the nurse. She asked if I still wanted to go ahead with the scan, but I said yes just to be on the safe side. And there our baby was, still lying there inside my now empty womb. There was nothing more the fertility clinic could do for us, we had to be referred back to hospital to manage the miscarriage as there would be a risk of infection after all this time from the dead tissue (my baby). At the hospital we sat in the same waiting room as we had for fertility appointments, and next to other pregnant women. We got marched down into the antenatal clinic where there were many pregnant women waiting for their scans. She ushered us into a quiet corner away from them and told us to wait. Another scan revealed exactly what the scan earlier that day had.

Back on the Women's Health Unit and eventually a nurse called me through to a room and handed me a leaflet titled 'Management of Miscarriage' and told me to read through the different options to discuss with the doctor.

Out of all those options I thought the best one would be to have an 'Evacuation of the Products of Reproduction' without anaesthetic as it had the fastest recovery times, and was likely to leave the least scarring as I didn't want to do anything to reduce the chances for our second embryo any more than they were. The doctor looked at me in horror. She'd looked at my notes and thought the best thing would be medical management, but without the tablet to induce bleeding as I'd lost so much blood the night before. I agreed to come in the following day to have the pessaries which would open up my cervix and let the baby pass.

I stayed in the hospital for ten hours with Rob by my side, with pessaries every couple of hours. Nothing. In fact the only thing my body seemed to want to let go of was the actual pessaries themselves.

They let us go again, with an appointment in a further two weeks to check if the baby had passed. At this stage if the 'tissue' was still present, then there would be no choice but to operate.

Week 12 - August 28 - two days before the scan I got up to go to the loo one morning, completely unexpectedly, quickly and without any pain at all the baby passed. Grey, and the size of a large raspberry. It went into the toilet before I even realised what it was. I knew for sure that was it. And I cried.

That was the end. On August 30 2013 I finally got the confirmation that my short lived but truly precious pregnancy was fully over.

No one really wanted to acknowledge that little life which meant everything to me from the moment I knew they existed. The grief carried on for months and to be honest, it never really leaves you.

It was a baby to us though, and I decided they needed to have a name. I would never know if they would have been a baby boy or a baby girl so I opted for Charlie. We held a blessing for our close family at a local church and it gave us a little closure.

Charlie was our dreams come true. He or she gave us hope when there was none, and with the end of their life also came the end of our hopes. Their life has touched my life forever and will never be forgotten. I will always feel like I let them down, no matter what and I'm so, so sorry for that. I love Charlie and I always will. I can only ever imagine what things could have been, and how their life could have turned out.

During our grief, Rob wrote this poem. I suppose for him it was a way for him to grieve and make sense of it all. He wanted to share it with you as part of Charlie's story.

A HEARTBEAT NO MORE

I saw you there
Clear as day
On the screen
Not human
But alive
And your heart was beating

Beating fast
You filled our world with joy
And happiness
We'd waited so long for this moment
We were alive
And our hearts were racing

She carried you for seven weeks
Taking care of you
And herself
I spoke to you and kissed your tomb
Praying you were alive
And that your heart was still beating

I never saw you again
You were never meant to be
Your mother spoke to me
The unthinkable
You were no longer alive
And your heart had stopped beating

I raced towards you
But it was too late
The devastation was deep rooted
I have never known such pain
I wish you were still alive
And that your heart was still beating

Now it is cold
The world seems dim
Your mother and I are hurting
I hope wherever you are you're ok
I know you will never be alive
And that your heart will beat no more

Rob and Nicola Hall

Jack

On the 29th January 2013 we went to the hospital for an urgent scan as I could not feel our (usually very active) baby boy move.

We were given the devastating news that our baby son's heart had stopped beating. The exact words used by the Sonographer will forever haunt me 'it's not going to be good news today'.... My memories of the next few days/weeks/hours are rather blurry (maybe my brains way of protecting me, perhaps too painful to recall).

What I do know is that our little boy Jack Holt was born fast asleep on 30.01.13 at 38 weeks gestation after a short - drug induced labour. Our beautiful boy weighed 6 pounds exactly. He had a little bit of fluffy blonde hair and a cute button nose.

He is big brother to Ava Grace and son of Adam and Susan Holt.

Our lives will never be the same without our little boy he was so wanted, so loved and will always be a massive part of our lives.

****

Little poem written for Jack by his Mummy and read by the graveside at his funeral:

Empty cot, shattered dreams
Tears falling down in streams

Unworn clothes and tiny socks
Memories of you kept safe in a box

Night night Jack, so perfect, so sweet
The Angels will keep you safe until the day we meet.

****

Sue & Adam Holt

Emma-Jane

Emma - Jane Faith Hope.

An angel that didn't have a chance of being here with us, that had to leave us far too soon.

Why God had to force me to make such a horrible decision like that is not fair but I know she is safe with the angels, back where she belongs.

Until we meet again and when her heart is fixed again, sleep tight princess.

We all miss you every day but I know you are watching over us all.

xxxx

Lisa Shaw & Douge Turner

Isla – Grace

Jacob

Travis Peter

Lucy Elizabeth

Jesse

Baby Steveson

Henry

This is my story about my beautiful baby boy Henry who was born sleeping on the 16th August 2015 at 2.53am.

Henry arrived early, at 21 weeks and 5 days, which was a devastating shock. An early arrival wasn't expected at all because at 20 weeks, a week and a half earlier, my scan at the hospital had been absolutely fine. Henry was moving around and his general health was really good.

I started having early contractions really late on during the night, just going into the morning. My waters shortly went afterwards and he seemed to be on his way. I was seen straight away at Chesterfield Royal Hospital and from it all happening at home, to being seen by the midwives and doctors, panic started to set in. I prayed Henry would be able to be saved somehow.

Unfortunately because of Henry's gestation he wasn't big enough or strong enough and he couldn't be saved. As I look back it took around an hour to deliver my beautiful angel into the world. I delivered Henry into the world at 2.53am and I remember those first moments like yesterday, as he was passed to me in a towel, just the same as if he had been born alive, which meant a lot. Henry was absolutely beautiful, just exactly how I pictured he would be when you imagine it in your head.

I moved into the bereavement room afterwards which was a bit more home from home. It had a double bed with bright bedding, a table, TV, shower and a rocking chair. Henry's footprints, handprints and weight were taken. He weighed only 430g.

Henry didn't have any clothes that would fit because of his size, he was so dainty and fragile yet so precious and beautiful. The midwife found a little blue knitted gown and a hat for him and a tiny little cotton nappy that came with a teddy. This was perfect for Henry. After he was dressed, he was laid inside a Moses basket on a stand with lovely blankets, and the basket was placed next to the bed to keep him safe and close by.

The next few days seemed to pass by in a blur, people coming to see me, consultants and midwives coming in and out, and it wasn't long before it was time to come home. Henry went for a post mortem as I was so upset and needed closure as to what happened and why things started to go wrong.

The planning started for Henry's funeral and flowers were ordered. 'SON' was spelt out in letters and a gorgeous flower spray was ordered to go on the top of his coffin. The weather on the day was cold, wet and murky. The sky cried with us all that day. Henry was laid to rest and we held a small wake for him after, which looking back was sad but also a lovely little send off for him.

Henry's bed is in a beautiful baby garden and the cemetery is so peaceful to visit and relaxing. I have some quiet time with him there as well as remembering him at home as well.

Henry's post mortem results came back that he passed away due to a blood clot behind my placenta and slight placenta abruption. I try not to blame myself but it's hard not to, as I always wonder if there was anything I could have done. I've been told that I would never have known as sadly it isn't possible to look behind the placenta on an ultrasound scan.

Henry is loved and missed so much by his family and friends and has touched the hearts of many people, and he is remembered and missed every single day. Henry's short life to 21 weeks gestation has taught me that life is precious and we should treasure every single day with our loved ones.

Thank-you for reading my story.

Marie Needham

Leona Marie

Baby Cowdrey

Zowie Louise

Caleb George

Caleb George Hooton was born sleeping on Monday 11th July 2016 at 7.35pm.

He is a much loved and missed son, brother, grandson, nephew and cousin.

Caleb weighed 8lb 4oz, was 55cms tall and was the double of his big sister Thea. He had lots of dark brown hair too.

He was born four days early after a low risk pregnancy. We went into hospital after I'd had contractions for two hours and heartbreakingly we were told there wasn't a heartbeat. I had noticed that his foot hadn't kicked my ribs since the Thursday before but had plenty of movements so didn't think anything of it.

They think there was a probable abruption of the placenta which led to a massive bleed and blood exchange to happen between us. The placenta was sent off to be examined and came back with no real abnormalities so they think that the membrane wall of the placenta gave way. There is no way of knowing how long the bleed was going on for as I didn't have any pains or bleeding. We only know how big the bleed was as I had to have almost three litres of Anti D to counteract Caleb's positive blood type cells in my negative blood.

Since Caleb's death four months ago, his parents, Tom and Ciara have raised almost £5000 for Sands and Tommy's charities.

'There is no footprint too small that cannot leave an imprint in this world'

Ciara and Tom

Tia Rose

Poppy

I was really chuffed when David asked me to write a short passage for his book.

Mine and my boyfriend's world was turned upside down nearly a year ago now. Everything was fine and then we went to our final scan. There was complete silence after being told there was no heartbeat. Still to this day, it's like my whole world had just stopped. I remember looking at my boyfriend and just thinking I had failed.

With time I have managed to deal with it, but you never ever forget.

David has done so much for all these beautiful babies featured in this book, and I am absolutely touched to be a part of it. Thank you so much David, for carrying our Angel Poppy and all the other Angels x

Anonymous

Ryan Aaron

William Roy

Ashley

Ruby Jayne

Aaron

Sasha

Flyn

CHESTERFIELD SANDS - THE STORY SO FAR..............

Chesterfield Sands support group was launched on March 26th 2011. After the loss of my daughter in 2010, I found there to be no support, help or counselling offered after the loss of a baby. I left hospital with empty arms and nothing else.

Over the next few months I stumbled across SANDS online and joined their forum, seeking help and support from other families that understood how I felt. The thought of other parents, younger parents going through what I had gone through, and worse, was unimaginable to me, and the thought of having to travel as far as Derby for my nearest support group was daunting, so I contacted Sands to see if I could set up a Sands group in Chesterfield. I was told that I couldn't do it alone so I posted on the Sands forum and facebook to find other bereaved parents to help, and 3 wonderful ladies volunteered.

So after months of planning and endless meetings and with the amazing help and support from Louisa Evans of Derby Sands, myself, Emma Sheppard, Stacey Haslam and Sharon Crossley were informed by Sands that we could launch Chesterfield Sands. After standing outside BHS stores to launch our group, with a static cycle and a couple of collection tubs we were underway.

The main Sands office warned us that it may be a few months before anyone attended our support group, but as we sat in the room for our very first meeting, the doors slowly opened and our first bereaved parent walked in. From then on, many families have stepped through those doors, some for one time only, some still attend today, but each family and each baby is remembered to this day.

In our first 5 years our group has provided a monthly support meeting every month without fail, and to this day providing support to bereaved families has always been and is our priority.

In our first 5 years, with the help of our local community, local bereavement services and the generosity of our friends, families and fundraisers we have raised enough funds to provide our local community and hospital with the following:

- The Never Land Baby Garden and memorial (Brimington Crematorium)
- Boythorpe Baby Garden and memorial (Boythorpe Cemetery)
- 2 Cuddle Cots
- Bed/Furniture/Equipment for Chesterfield Birth Centre's bereavement suite
- Memorial Services at Christmas and on Baby Loss Awareness Day(Wave of Light)

During this time we have had support as Sainsbury's charity of the year, and have held many fundraising events to raise awareness and funds for these projects. Local bereaved parents have done the most amazing fundraising including sponsored walks, runs, mud runs, colour runs, cycles, climbs, swims, skydives, bungee jumps, motorcycles, slims, ironman comps, extreme walks, music nights, fun days, cake sales, fancy dress, coffee mornings, charity balls, charity stalls, craft stalls and sooo much more. We cannot thank each and every person enough for helping, supporting and donating, we are so very grateful.

Over the past 2 1/2 years, Chesterfield Sands has emerged and grown with a fantastic committee who give so much time and effort to make this group the group it is today. Thank you to Emma Sheppard, Louise Hopkinson, Claire Cadman,

Donna Elliott and Zoë Venables for their dedication and hard work all given voluntarily. We have also met some amazing fundraisers including David Smith and his family. David has not only raised thousands of pounds for us, not only taken our babies on all his travels, he has also inspired us, supported us and taught us that anything is possible if we just try. We are humbled and so very grateful to you David.

Not only do we do these silly events to raise money and awareness but to make memories for our babies, to remember them and to do them proud. We now have a baby banner with the names of over 200 babies which we take to all our events far and wide. We are always welcoming new people to come along and join us in our events, the more the merrier!!

We may not be trained counsellors but we know something all those professionals don't.......we KNOW how it feels to lose a baby. We understand the pain, the anger, the emptiness and all the feelings that come with such devastation. And we all find our own way to live with it each day. We support anyone affected by the loss of a baby at any stage of pregnancy, during or after birth and however recent or long ago. We are here to help.

Thank you for taking time to read about our group.

Nicky Whelan – Chesterfield Sands Chair

CHESTERFIELD SANDS GROUP INFORMATION

What are our aims?
SANDS Aims and objectives are as follows…….
We have 3 core aims:
WE SUPPORT ANYONE AFFECTED BY THE DEATH OF A BABY
Bereavement support is at the core of everything we do. Some of the services that we offer include:

- Helpline for parents, families, carers and health professionals
- UK-wide network of support groups with trained befrienders
- Online forum and message boards enabling bereaved families to connect with others
- Website and a wide range of leaflets, books and other resources.
-

WE WORK IN PARTNERSHIP WITH HEALTH PROFESSIONALS TO TRY TO ENSURE THAT BEREAVED PARENTS AND FAMILIES RECEIVE THE BEST POSSIBLE CARE

We deliver bereavement care training for professionals across the UK. The parents' experience is central to each workshop. Our training is skills focused and evidence based to ensure professionals gain the insight, understanding and knowledge to confidently provide sensitive bereavement care for parents when a baby dies. Sands also offers support to professionals affected by the death of a baby.

WE PROMOTE AND FUND RESEARCH THAT COULD HELP TO REDUCE THE LOSS OF BABIES' LIVES

In spite of medical advances, the shocking reality is that 5712 babies were stillborn or died within the first 28 days of life in 2013. We raise funds for and support vital research, whilst working in partnership with Government and key stakeholders to address these individual tragedies as a matter of urgency and priority.

What does our group provide?

We hold monthly support meetings to give bereaved families and chance to meet others and to talk in a safe friendly environment with others that understand and care. We offer/give support through our social media pages and private facebook group. We provide telephone and email support to those that may not want/can't attend group meetings. We will also meet on a one to one basic for those that would benefit. We provide memorial services for our bereaved families so they can remember their babies in a special way. We also have support literature in the form of leaflets, and books written by bereaved parents that we loan out on a library type system. We support families locally and other areas including Sheffield, Doncaster, Rotherham, Retford, Matlock and Worksop.

How to find us……
Support Meetings:
1st Tuesday of every month
7.00-9.00pm
Community Room, Chesterfield Community Fire Station,
Spire Walk Business Park,
Braidwood Way,
Chesterfield. S40 2WH.
(off the Hornsbridge roundabout, behind B&Q)

Helpline number: 07432387725

E-mail – chesterfieldsands@gmail.com
https://www.facebook.com/chesterfield.sands.5
https://www.facebook.com/chesterfieldsands
https://twitter.com/Chfieldsands

Joshua B Ebony Jessica W Sienna W Noel & James Joel Kaiden H Archie & Raife Rebekka Dotty Jaden Emma L-J Austyn Alexei Elsa Jordan Hannah Baby Adams Ben Paige-Elizabeth & Lola-Emily Riley Christopher W Bethani-Beryl Scarlett Matthew Danielle Abigail H Daniel H Caleb William N Joseph W Aimee Jo Antonia Roman Benjamin J & Harry J Willow Brogan Mia Lucy Baby Stevenson Zoie Dylan Elizabeth B Regan T Mason Freddie H Ethan & Issac Jacob Bella & Baby B Teegan W & Baby Woods Charlie Sam Angel-Precious Beanie Freya H Jacob H Malakai James & Charlie G Baby Edwards Sam B Jacob O'C Jock Bethie Harry W Sam Ollie Podge Henry Faith Ezra Joseph O Pip Cooper Leah Kobi-Kai Lillie-Rae & 4 Angels Ashton Cameron Robin Isaac Logan T Paul Baby Sharpe Lucy E Jack A Niamh Ella Amy Harper Luke Lily W Adam & Baby King Poppy V & Baby V Archie Isla Gabriel Violet Oliver Zizi Theo Ian Aimee Joel & Kieran Charlie Jak & Harrison Lillie-Grace & Baby Boo Thomas Charlie H Rosie Alex Lucy R Lily R Samuel A Evangeline Theo C Ava Frankie W Bella-Mai Declan-Nathaniel Georgia-Lauren Nevaeh-Aaliyah Lexi-Lei Isabel H-C & Baby H-C Shanice Baby Ahmed Esmae C Lola Joan Finley-Kai Owen Baby McCracken Bobby PH Teegan Phoenix J Olly & Lewis Kylie Mason Ruby & Lola Réiltín & Seren James K Ashley H Louise W Kenzie-Joe Leona-Marie George Cory Harmony & Angel Rubyjayne Nicole James P Eric Milly H Sams Angels & Paige H Baby Sevante Angel Walsh Jayson Ryan & Kyle Indie Aubs Korban Lucas R Tia & Ryan Xander Emma C & Andrew C Connor Kiara Isabella T George M Harriet Oliver P Isla-Grace Casey-Leigh Jassy & Nathaniel Benjamin J & Emily J Oliver S Lauren & Brandon Hollie & Ethan Baby Newton Kinley Baby Bear Amy R Essie Baby Owen Robyn & Marlai Ernie Baby F & Baby Fleming Travis D Bethany-Grace Robbie S Lila Orsino Jamie C & Charlie C Baby Cowdrey Freddie B Leigha-Jade & Amiee-Grace Aaron Sasha Thomas P Milly Elliot Evelyn Annie

Remembering All Other Babies Taken Too Soon

Acknowledgements

I have so many people to thank in writing this book that I apologise if I miss someone out, but here goes.

Theo, my second grandson. Without you none of this story would have happened. We would never have found SANDS and there would never have been any Angel Poles. Look over your Mummy and keep her safe.

My late father, who loved the written word and tried to instill his passion and creativity into me. I should have taken more notice, Dad. He also taught me there is no such word as "can't" and if you try hard enough nothing is impossible. He was a wise man indeed.

Mark Cameron, author of "The diary of an average runner aged 41 and a half", who showed me how easy it is to publish your own e-book.

Catherine and Drew for having the arduous task of trying to proof read my ramblings. You must be brain dead by now. I really appreciate your efforts.

Graeme and Toby from 'popi' who very kindly designed the book cover. I recommend their services to you. www.popi.co.uk

The great athletes I have competed with and suffered with over the years. You have pushed me to, and beyond, my limits and shown me nothing is impossible. Without your help and encouragement and navigational skills I would not have completed many of the events I entered.

Peter Smith for sacrificing your Triathlon X race to help me. Without your selfless act I would not have been able to get the baby banner to the top of Scafell Pike. You were the true winner of the triathlon.

The staff and customers of the pharmacy I work in at Dronfield. You have dug into your pockets and generously supported my charities for many years and I am eternally grateful. You really have made a difference to the lives of many people.

All my friends at Ashgate Hospice, the Chesterfield MS Society and Chesterfield SANDS. Many of you deal with situations I can't even imagine, on a daily basis with such courage and determination. You are a true inspiration and I am truly proud to support you.

Nicky, the chair of Chesterfield SANDS. I have hounded you constantly, asking you to post numerous articles on the SANDS Facebook page over the last 2 years. You always manage to oblige, even though you have a busy life to live.

The Pole Angel families who appeared on my poles and shared their stories here. It must have stirred up a multitude of emotions. I thank you for your bravery.

My beautiful wife Ann, who has put up with me for the last 16 years. You are always there to help, support, encourage, advise, listen and find all the things I lose. You battle the symptoms of MS every day without moaning or making excuses. You have given me the best 16 years of my life. I know I am a lucky guy.

Stop wishing. Start doing – author unknown